Some were Patriots ~ Some were Prodigals

One of msbev's Heritage Books . . . .
As msbev remembers

A "seasoned" Storyteller, msbev writes some of the stories she has told over the years. A love of history and family are combined in little book. Don't be surprised if you laugh or cry at times. You will be reminded of your own family. It has been said we must not amputate our history; it helps us define our destiny . . .

Some were Patriots ~ Some were Prodigals

Stories From the Heart by msbev Volume 1

Beverly Brown Hart

authorHOUSE®

AuthorHouse™ LLC
1663 Liberty Drive
Bloomington, IN 47403
www.authorhouse.com
Phone: 1-800-839-8640

Published by AuthorHouse   10/09/2013

ISBN: 978-1-4918-2108-4 (sc)
ISBN: 978-1-4918-2109-1 (e)

Library of Congress Control Number: 2013917741

Dedicated

to

Max R Hart Sr. 1942-2009

Contents

Bits and Pieces.. 1

Genealogy Begins! 3

Msbev remembers the Summer of 1966 ~ A 15 pound baby?......... 17

It is "just a dog"... 29

The Year was 1958 A Politician Came to visit . . . .

    We lived in a shotgun house 39

The Year was 1961 ~ It was a Runaway Tractor?............................. 43

GLIMPSES OF DAD'S FAMILY

Polly's Hero ~ Patriot or Prodigal?..................................... 51

Jum Meets a Lady from Arkansas...................................... 59

Simply . . . . Calvin Brown... 65

These Things I Remember about my Dad 71

GLIMPSES OF MOTHER'S FAMILY

Flood Water were a'rising And the baby was a'coming..................... 75

The Betty Jean Story 81

NO! It Isn't an Ice Cream Dish 93

Anthony Casey and Louisa Richards ~ Happiness after

    the Uncivil War 101

There is a Panther On the Mountain.................................. 109

A Woman Plain and Simple She Kept a Secret for 40 years............ 117

These Things I Remember About Mama 133

A Bit more 139

Illustrations

Max Jr, Justin... 24
Max, Bev 13,48,49,58,77,78,82,88
Dec 02 1886 newspaper.. 14
Arthur Brown 24,82,100
Frankie Casey Brown.. 58,100
John Wesley Brown 56,57
Victoria Brown 58
Lula Triplett... 58
Calvin Brown 69
Lonnie Brown... 58,79
Howard Brown 58,79
Howard pencil drawing.. 90
McCutcheon Cave Creek... 89
Margaret Houston Casey.. 91,129
Frankie Casey Country school... 98
Class Newton Co Academy.. 99
Newton Co AR. Buffalo Church... 106
Buffalo Church 107,108
Harvey Houston 127,128
Magazine pic A Lincoln Family.. 126
Harriett Blackwood Houston 128
Jesse and Margaret Casey... 129
W C Houston Chancel AR.. 130
Letter to Margaret Houston Casey... 131
Newton County Academy pic... 141
Mother's make do pin cushion various... 147
Old Alluwe artifacts.. 149

Introduction

I listened patiently for answers to my questions. Few came. At times mother simply looked at me; as though willing me to stop asking questions. She told me as much by what she did not say as what she did.

This is not about great accomplishments {although there are great ones.} Some of these folks just could not rise above the forces which tugged on them.

Johan Hounshell (spelled various) was born in Germany @ 1730. Almost 300 years have passed. His decision to come to America and begin a new life has allowed me to enjoy living as an American. How do you thank someone for that?

I am the only daughter (and youngest child) of a blacksmith-farmer born in Indian Territory near Old Alluwe. Mother shared information sparingly. Mama was raised near the Buffalo River in Newton Co AR. Her family was among the early settlers of the early 1800s. I have learned more of what they overcame to give each of us more of what they could not have.

Ohhh, yes Mother and Dad were among the patriots. First, Dad was a prodigal.

The smoky, foggy hills of Arkansas somehow call to me. I walk out into my Okla yard at the first hint of dawn, to smell the new day God has prepared. I have been known to drive into the countryside to see the fields at early dawn wearing their morning coat of dew or frost. The early morning haze reminds me of the beautiful valley near Parthenon, AR where mother grew up. I would tell my husband, "ohh, this is an Arkansas Morning!"

His only comment was "If you say so, mom, if you say so." He knew what I meant, as always.

I work part time from my home. I owned Sooner Tax Service down town for 20+ years before semi retiring. I am an Enrolled Agent doing payroll and income tax returns. Being semi-retired means I organize stories I have written over the years and travel to tell a Story. I am known as msbev, the Storyteller.

A special thank you to Diana Cecil and Cindy McWilliams. These ladies are cousins by birth and choice. Diana and Cindy made it possible for our family to be included as descendants of the patriot Johan Casper Hounshell. I was accepted into the Daughters of American Revolution in 2012.

I remember 40+ years ago a conversation I had with my dad, Arthur Brown. I had been asking questions . . . again! He thought I was "fighting a losing battle". He told me, "Betty, you will never find anything about the Browns"

Brother, Lonnie, and I chuckle as we ponder the look on dad's face if he were here. He would be so pleased. Only one person would be more pleased, my husband."

This is my first "Heritage" book to write. I can go no further without acknowledging the man whose encouragement and support knew no bounds. I was 16 when I married him; 48 years was not quite long enough but I will see him again. Heaven is not a myth. Heaven is real.

Thank you, my dear husband who passed to Glory before me. Love truly does come softly.

Some of us Were Patriots
Some of us Were Prodigals

Volume I

A Long Journey

1752 Germany

Pennsylvania

Virginia

Kentucky

Missouri

Arkansas

Indian Nations

Oklahoma

Bits and Pieces

I really remember only "bits and pieces" of my childhood. Perhaps this is because I did such a small share of the work, being the youngest. I thought it to be quite a good arrangement.

I remember a little of moving. The zinc bathtub would be brought in to the house. Mama would begin filling it. Lots of fruit jars would go into that tub. Every tub and bucket and basket would be used to move. These were loaded on to the back of the truck.

I remember when we heard the news. The government was putting a dam on the river. It would be called the Oologah Dam. Our house would be under water when the rains came. We had to move. It would be difficult for mother. But, hadn't most things been? I mean, had not most things been difficult for her? She didn't complain. Her life had been filled with hard work, at least since she married.

Mother had been raised to have a home which was as nice as most of the homes in the little valley where she lived While her dad was not rich, he had managed to have a comfortable home for his daughters. When mother's mom became ill, her papa took mama to the Mayo Clinic. The doctors could not do anything for Margaret . . . beautiful, beautiful, Margaret. She died slowly. Doctors called it a goiter. It was on her neck and it would get bigger. It did. Mother was 9 years old when her mama died. Mother was lonely but she had a loving father and older sisters. Mother lived in a little valley where many of the families were related to her. That is not too hard to understand when you realize her papa was one of 23 children sired by William Uriah Casey.

One day when dad was in a thoughtful mood he talked of the early days of their marriage. He told how cold it was in the little house where they used to live. The house was little more than a shack. He said they pulled the old metal bed close to the stove; but when morning came they would still shake snow off the quilt! He would go to the field and when he returned mother would be back in bed! Though the years had passed, I could sense the frustration in his voice. How would this little woman ever adapt to the hardships of the Oklahoma river bottom to which he had brought her?

"Work to be done and your mama piled up back in the bed", he said. Many years had passed and the wonder of their survival showed in his voice.

I silently wondered if that was the only place she could ease the bitter cold from her body. Survive is what they did. Those times were such that I cannot imagine.

This collection of stories reflects some of those stories I heard. I admit, at times, I coaxed and pleaded for more stories. I was never satisfied!

Being born the youngest of three children, I missed some of those life experiences which shaped those early days of marriage. Their responses to my endless questions are the foundation of much of what follows.

Some of the stories are as factual as I know how to tell them. Others are enhanced. You will know the difference. Remember the words of Will Rogers who once said, "How can you trust a fellow who can spell a word only one way?" . . . Or was that Mark Twain? . . . or was it Ms. Bev?

Genealogy Begins!

My father was Arthur T Brown, born at Old Alluwe, Indian Territory. He was born a few months before Oklahoma entered into the Union. His parents were John Wesley and Victoria Arella Tilton Brown.

Victoria Arella Tilton Brown, born Jan 12, 1890, was the daughter of Joseph and Mary Adams Tilton.

My mother was Frankie Casey, the daughter of Jesse Columbus Casey and Margaret Houston Casey. Mother was born in 1912 and lived in Newton County, Arkansas until she moved to Oklahoma. Mother and dad, Arthur T Brown, were married in the Methodist Church at Old Alluwe, OK on Christmas Eve 1931.

My grandparents, John Wesley {Wes} and Victoria were parents of 6 children who lived past infancy. Arthur was the oldest born in 1907. Next is Teddy Alfored who was born and died in 1908. Joseph Harmon was born 1910, Lula Brown Triplett born 1915, Mary Fannie Brown Quigley born 1920, Pauline Brown born 1922 and Denis McElery Brown born 1932,

John Wesley {Wes} Brown was born Feb 13, 1879 in Ray County, Missouri and came to the Indian Nations prior to statehood. We are still learning about the Brown Family. My dad, Arthur, was 6 ft 4 inches tall and he said, "The old man was taller than me." He estimated his dad to be about 6 ft. 7 inches tall. On Wes' WWI registration card he stated he worked for Bob Lee at his General Store in Alluwe, Okla. Wes was a "loner" most of his life. He trapped and hunted and traveled by boat up and down the Verdigris River.

Dad told me that his dad, Wes Brown, had pearl handled revolvers. I never saw them and do not know what happened to them.

I was not around Wes at all. I told mother that I remembered seeing my grandfather, Wes Brown, one time. She said, "I don't think so."

I was 7 years old when Wes died but I really do not ever remember going to visit him. I told mother I did remember seeing him one time. She asked when that would have been.

"Well, we had gone to Grandma Brown's house in Chelsea. I was walking around the red truck. I saw this man leaning up against the outside of Grandma Brown's house. I remember thinking he was as tall as the house! "Probably I was looking up at such an angle it seemed that his head was almost touching the eave of the roof.

Mother thought about it and finally said, "Well, I guess maybe you do remember seeing him."

I saw Grandma Brown occasionally. She lived in Chelsea, OK in a little two room house just a couple of blocks off highway 66. She grew a big garden and had the most gorgeous rose moss growing in enamel pans in her back yard. The honeysuckle on the side grew out of bounds. I loved it! I remember her grass was always cut and trimmed so neatly. She mowed it with a push reel mower; and did it very well. You see, Grandma had a stroke when her youngest child, Dennis, was six weeks old. She kept one arm close to her side, but she was a spunky little woman. She had large eyes that sparkled when she looked at you.

My cousin, Arella Quigley Lewis, told me that she stayed with Grandma Brown quite a bit when she was growing up. She remembers grandma insisting they go to bed when it got dark. They rose early in the morning, before daylight. Grandma did not want to "burn electricity" when it wasn't necessary. No need to "waste" electricity. I think Grandma must have felt that electricity in the morning was less expensive than electricity at night (?) I remember Grandma Brown baking the most wonderful custard pie.

My dad called his mother "ma". She was such a tiny little thing and he was such a big man; I wondered if she pondered that she gave birth to such a good sized child. I never asked.

I was 12 years old when Grandma Brown died. Grandma Brown was walking the few blocks from her little house to down town Chelsea when she fell over near the railroad tracks. Her parents were Joseph and Mary Tilton.

Grandpa Brown {Wes} was at Eastern State Hospital in Vinita when he fell and died shortly thereafter. I understand he suffered from dementia.

I was not told that Grandpa and Grandma Brown divorced. Another researcher told me she found the divorce record not realizing I had never been told. I knew they did not live together. Bless their hearts. Wish I had known them "more"; but I honor their memory by placing flowers at the cemetery on Memorial Day. I have done this for almost 40 years. First, my husband helped me and I will continue to do this as long as I am able to make the drive. Victoria is buried at Chelsea City Cemetery. Wes is buried at Nowata City Cemetery.

Dad and Mother remained in Craig County while Wes was in Eastern State Hospital. We lived east of Vinita, OK for about 3 years. This was in the early 1950's. Dad worked on a ranch and was away part of the time "following the Harvest". We lived in a house which was on the ranch property. I remember the man who lived across the road offered me something to drink from his refrigerator. I wasn't too sure about this. I was about 4 years old. Mother urged me to try it; she said I would like it. It was red water, but I finally took a sip. I had never tasted anything like that. Mother said it was called Kool-Aid. It was sooo good!

While we lived there I remember Jack Inman from Nowata coming to visit. I liked Mr. Inman as he always gave me a coin when he was leaving. He smiled at dad and me. Mr. Inman ran a ranch or horse business of some type. Even though I was small, I knew the two men respected each other. That was a good thing.

While we lived in this house I began first grade at Afton, OK. Still remember the wonderful teacher. Her name was Myrtle Hubbard. Ms. Hubbard had never married. She was sooo nice. I remember missing the Christmas party at school as I was sick with the chicken pox.

Brother Lonnie went to two country schools. He attended Todd School in 5th grade and Success School in 6th grade. I remember one of the teachers driving her model A and picking up Lonnie to give him a ride to school. I asked Lonnie if he remembered the day I tried to ride to school with him. He said he did not remember.

I just knew if I could get in that car, I could go to school. I had a "plan". After all these years, I still remember "my plan"; this is my first memory of wanting to go to school. I was 4 years old. After all these years I remain in awe of education and the doors it can open.

There was a large tree near the edge of our yard. I would stand behind the tree, when the lady stopped her car, I would run and get in the car. That morning Mrs. Shearhart came and stopped the car. I did as I planned. Mother did not fit into my plan. She lifted me from the car. I had to wait to go to school. I was sad and cried. I do not remember mother scolding me severely. She must have secretly sympathized with her little daughter!

Brother Howard went to school at Afton. He played football. Howard was very intelligent and nice looking. I began first grade the year after oldest brother graduated from high school.

We moved back to Nowata County on what mother and dad called the "Van Winkle Place". This is because they rented the buildings and acreage from Ferman Van Winkle.

When Oologah Dam was built we had to move. Dad was able to purchase 40 acres on highway 60 thinking he would build a house there. Property became available for purchase just across the road which had a small shotgun house on it. He purchased the 10 acres as well. We would live in it until dad purchased a house and had it moved in.

We moved only a couple of miles away but it was outside Nowata School District. Lonnie could drive and was able to drive into town where he would graduate in 1957.

I was in 7th grade and no longer in Nowata School District so I went to a one room schoolhouse a mile away. It was called Armstrong School. I didn't know what to think. There were 8 grades in one room. I look back with awe and thankfulness. What a neat experience. I really did walk one mile to school every day. The teacher was Mrs. Hobbs. Mother and Dad had known her for years. Her son in law was Mr. Inman who used to visit us when we lived east of Vinita.

After going to Armstrong I finished the 8th grade and went to high school at Alluwe. The Alluwe bus came by the house. While going to school at Alluwe I met a boy who was driving out from Nowata. He needed a class in order to graduate. The class was not being offered at Nowata that semester. I began dating him and married Max in 1962.

More about my Dad's Family

Dad's father was John Wesley (Wes) Brown. Wes' parents were Andrew Jackson Brown and Martha Fields {m1. Mr. Mattocks} Brown. Martha or Mattie had children from her first marriage; Martha, Elizabeth and Cynthia. Andrew and Mattie had 1, John Wesley Brown, 2. Matilda Frances Brown, 3. Calvin Brown and 4. Octavia Brown.

Martha Fields Mattocks' parents were Stephen Fields and Mariam McDonald.

Andrew Jackson Brown's parents were John and Matilda Jane Carter Brown. John and Matilda Jane Brown were married in 1841 in Smythe Co, VA We know of 5 children: 1.Andrew Jackson Brown, 2. Lurinda Brown m. George Shelly; 3. Thomas Jefferson Brown m. Sarah Frances McCullough, 4. Columbia Francis Brown; 5. Joseph Calvin m. Amanda Sisk.

John Brown's parents were Isham and Christina Hounshell Brown. Isham was born about 1792 in Virginia. Isham and Christina were married about 1815, Isham and Christina moved from Virginia to Kentucky where both died. Isham died several years before Christina. Christina lived part of the time with Peter Brown, her son. Christina Hounshell Brown died July 17, 1875 in Boyd Co, KY of stomach cancer.

Isham and Christina reared a large family. The oldest is my ancestor, John Brown b. 1817 in VA. Next are Hiram, Wesley, Henry, Isham

Jr, Peter, Lavisa Brown Wilcox, James W Brown, and Joseph Brown. Isham and Christina purchased and sold land in Kentucky. Isham and Christina are not on the 1850 census; so we must assume they were traveling and were missed by the census taker in 1850.

We are still searching for Isham's ancestors. I "think" Isham and a cousin both were born in VA and they both named their children similar names. Both of these men had descendants who went to Missouri. John and Matilda moved to Missouri. John moved back to Kentucky but Matilda remained in Missouri. Matilda lived with her daughter, Lurinda Shelly.

John moved back to Kentucky where he listed himself as a "widower" when he married a younger woman, Amanda Rucker. Of course, Matilda was still living in Missouri.

John drew up a will and left his children each twenty five cents.

I will leave the Brown lineage and; at this time, begin with the family of John Brown's mother, Christina Hounshell Brown.

Christina Brown's parents were Andrew Hounshell who married Louisa Lambert.

Christina Brown's grandparents were Johan Casper Hounshell who married Christina Messerschmidt "Messersmith".

Johan Casper Hounshell Family

Christina Hounshell was born Feb 28, 1796 to Andrew and Louisa Lambert Hounshell. Louisa was the daughter of Henry Lambert and Maria Magdalena Daude. Louisa was born Aug 30, 1766 in Dauphin Co PA and died Oct 19, 1802 in Wythe Co, VA.

Andrew Hounshell was born Oct 03, 1766 in Pennsylvania. He died about 1832 in Wythe Co, VA and is buried at St. Paul's Church at Crocket, VA. Andrew would have been a small boy, less than 10 years of age when his dad was listed as being a member of Virginia Militia. Andrew surely grew up in a home which "lived the REAL American

Dream"! Andrew was only 11 years old when his dad signed an Oath of Allegiance. No doubt the family stories abounded!

One reason I think so is the family naming pattern: Isham's son, John Brown, named his son Andrew Brown . . . probably to honor his {John's maternal grandfather, Andrew Hounshell}. Andrew Brown, born in VA in 1842. Named his son John Wesley Brown. John Wesley "Wes" was my grandfather. It goes like this:

Andrew Hounshell' s daughter>Christina Hounshell m. Isham Brown >John>Andrew>John Wesley>Arthur>Bev Brown hart

Andrew and Louisa were married Sep 17, 1786 in Montgomery Co, VA.

Andrew and Louisa had children; John Hounshell, Christina Hounshell, and Mary Hounshell.

Christina Hounshell married Isham Brown.{See preceding page}

Andrew's parents were Johan Casper Hounshell and Christina Messersmith.

Johan Casper Hounshell was born 1730 in Germany. He died Aug 01. 1810 in Wythe Co, VA.

Johan or John Casper Hounshell would have been about 22 years old when he left Germany to board a ship to arrive in this country. He married at 27 years of age. Christina was a couple of years older. Johan served his newly adopted country which meant he left Christina to care for their home often times without her husband to help her.

The ship, Queen of the Denmark arrived in Pennsylvania on Friday, Mar 3, 1752. On the ship's list is John Ohnshield. Many of the people spoke only broken English. 1.

Christina Messersmith was the daughter of Andreas Messerschmidt and Anna Heyes.

Christina was born before Oct 17, 1728 in Ofterdingen Baden~Wertemberg, Germany. She died Sept 01. 1798 in Wythe Co, VA.

Pastor Friedrich Schultz united John Haunshield and Christina Messerschmidt in marriage.

John Casper and Christina Hounshell were married 1757 in Montgomery Co, VA and had the following children: Andrew Hounshell m. Louisa Lambert; Major John Hounshell; Maria or Mary Elisabeth Hounshell; and Christina Hounshell.

1768 John Casper Hounshell was one of 31 residents of Reed Creek of Holston, Augusta Co, (later Wythe Co, VA.) who signed petition asking for an improvement to their Patent Lands.

1772—"A List of Tithables in Capt. Doacks and my own companies for year 1772 taken by Walter Crocket. List also includes John's brother in laws, John and Barnabas Messersmith. At bottom of list there are men listed who had more than one tithable. There is listed "John Ounshell:2" 1 this would be John Casper Hounshell and his son, (Major) John who was about 16 years old in 1773.

1773—There is a news item in the Virginia Gazette. Which lists Robert Doack as Representative for new county of Fincastle, Virginia. He would become John Hounshell's military commander within the year.

1774—Captain Robert Doack lists John Bunshell {Hounshell} as being in his militia company on June 2, 1774. Stated these men are Defenders of the Frontier; 2 but did not participate in the Battle of Point Pleasant. Captain Doack died in summer of 1774. John Bunshell {Hounshell} is listed between two of his brothers in law; John Messersmith and Barnet Messersmith.

Sept through Dec 1777; John Hounshell (his mark) was one of the men in newly formed Montgomery Co, VA who swore his allegiance before James McGavock. 1. John Casper Hounshell was about 47 years old

1782—John Houndshell and Barney Messersmith and Henry Lambert and Martin Wyrick listed at bottom of page with certain sum noted. {Author noted probably due to nearing age 50?} 1

1782—John Ownshull was taxed in Montgomery Co, VA. 2 tithable persons listed; no slaves. John Casper Hounshell was perhaps exempted from further military service in 1782 but not exempted from taxes. 1

A deed found in Wythe Co VA Deeds lists 113 acres sold to Lewis Kegley for $1.00. Land was sold by heirs of Johan Hounshell, dated Aug 11, 1810. 1

1886 Newspaper article indicating two of the Brown brothers are selling their land and moving to the Indian Nations to claim their birthright. Calvin and Thomas Jefferson Brown were brothers of Andrew Brown.

Where was their brother, Andrew Brown, my great great grandfather? I think he was in the Indian Nations waiting for his brothers to arrive.

Andrew's son, John Wesley Brown, {my grandfather} tells the census taker he was born in Missouri. Wes told his son, Arthur {my father} he was born near Old Alluwe Indian Territory. It could well be that he was born in Missouri and moved as a small tyke to Indian Nations. My dad said he (Arthur) was born at Old Alluwe Indian Territory a few months before Oklahoma became a state.

Evidently I did not "break the tradition" greatly. Best I can figure from what brother remembers; the family was living on "The Island" near Old Alluwe when I was born. Brother refers to it as The Hallum Place. He remembers one incident which evidently happened just before I was born. The island flooded often. The water evidently rose rapidly as well.

Lonnie said dad had been going down and checking the water depth frequently. After one such "check" things started to happen quickly. Lonnie was small, probably 6 or 7 years old. He remembers dad going to check the water; then he remembers being in a truck belonging to our uncle. Lonnie was riding in the cab with mother. As he looked outside, he could see water coming up between the slats in the wooden bridge as they crossed the bridge. Also, the water was getting really deep by the time they got across the bridge. He remembers how swift the water was running and even as young as he was; he remembers thinking they could be in "trouble" if they didn't get out of there and quick. He looked back to see dad and older brother, Howard, walking and driving livestock through the water! What a dangerous trip that must have been. This was before I was born. Mother and dad and brothers stayed with mother's sister's mother-in-law for a few days.

Lonnie remembers "playing" with Uncle Bill Denton's brother who was in a wheel chair. The two boys got along well, time passed quickly and mother and dad were able to return home.

This flooding episode must have been about all my pregnant mama could take. Shortly after my birth mother and dad moved west of Nowata near E J and Mamie Williams. The Williams and my parents would remain friends all their lives. Mamie never had any children. She had a doll with three faces. Mamie gave me the doll which I named Mamie. There is a knob on the top of the doll's head which will turn. There are three faces, awake, sleep and crying. I have taken it to elementary schools when I told a story. The doll never fails to create a lot of interest!

1. Allen Hounshell + Clifford Canfield authors of book "The Hounshells of SW Virginia
2. Beverly Brown Hart research
3. Next pg-Dec 2, 1886 Jeff and Cal Brown sell land to move to Indian NationsJeff Brown and Cal Brown sell farms as they are going to the Indian Nation, as they have a birthright there. Mid way down column heading EVERETT DEW DROPS

Max bev 1961 we are sitting on couch in Bev's parent's house

Dec. 2, 1886

Everett Items.

Weather somewhat winterish.

Christmas is fast approaching.

Taxpaying time is here, and nothing to pay with.

Cap. Scarce says his cattle will break him up. We feel for him, but can't reach him.

Wm. Reese left for Kansas City last Saturday.

People are fixing up their sleds and sleighs. They must be looking for snow.

Sausage are getting ripe around and about Everett.

On Tuesday night, the 23d, we saw a light in the M. E. church. No appointment, no bell rang, and it was a query in our mind what was up. We don't have to make suppers to pay for our house, but we are going at it now.

The Baptist Ladies Aid Society had a circle sewing on the 24th at Mr. Hudson's.

Elder Foster sold to Wm. Steen 14 head of steers, coming threes, at $3 25, averaging 263.

The Baptist froze out with their prayer meeting Wednesday night; the Methodist ate their's out on Thursday night, and turned it into an oyster supper.

Dr. Arnold sold his ducks, 30 in number.

Dr. Patten has returned from Dennis, Texas.

Isaac Wilcox was playing at school the other day and ran against the fence and knocked one tooth out and broke two off even with the gums.

Mrs. H. Stoke has been absent the past week in Bates county.

L. T. Dorsett's drawer that was stolen out of his safe nearly a year ago, was found on the 25th inst. in Wm. Reighngale's orchard, with day book and papers, but the $10 taken at the time was not there.

We are requested to state that there will be an oyster supper at the Baptist church in Everett on Christmas Eve, done by order of the committee which met on the 24th. All are invited to be present. There will be everything that can be had, to eat, and a Christmas tree free for the benefit of all.

We also learn there will be a supper at the M. E. church on the same night. If that is the case won't we have a big time and lots to eat.

EVERETT DEW DROPS.

Weather fine, roads good.

Health exceedingly good, except bad colds.

Big rain last Monday, the 22d last—a regular spring day thermometer, 70 deg. above; and since Tuesday it has ranged from 25 to 60 deg. above zero. We have not had any extreme cold weather yet.

A great many farmers are plowing their fallow land preparatory to early planting.

Cattle men have got down to earnest feeding, and their cattle looks well.

M. M. and George Cable, jr., and F. C. George landed from Kansas City last week with 156 head of three-year-olds, for which they gave three cents per pound.

F. M. George and Jno. French have added 86 head of cattle to their ranch.

Jeff Brown sold his farm to Richard Weatherholt, and Cal. Brown sold his farm of 120 acres to F. M. George for $2,500. The Browns are going to the Indian Nation, as they have a birthright there.

E. W. Longwell and S. E. Licklider have taken timber claims out in southwest Kansas. Licklider says he got on the top of Mr. Cook's house, who is now living in Finny county, Kans., (but formerly of Archie, this county,) and counted 324 dugouts and houses. Eph. Brown went with Licklider, and while they were there they had the pleasure of being in one of the Kansas blizzards. It did not take Eph.'s eye. While Licklider was out hunting a claim, Eph. decided to leave, and left S. E. a note, which read: "Not knowing when you will return, and as I am under expenses, I will return and bid adieu to the land of blizzards.

The Ladies aid society of the Baptist Church, of Everett, met on Wednesday, November 24th, and made arrangements for an old-fashioned supper, consisting of chicken, pies, cakes, meats, oysters and all other goodies. Supper to be served at the Baptist Church in Everett, on Friday night before Christmas, 1886, and in connection with the supper, the Sunday-school will give an entertainment in the form of a saxon house—substitute for a christmas tree. Santa Claus will be on his annual trip. Select songs; declamation and speeches will be among the entertainments. Committees are selected and everything is in running order. Admittance:

village blacksmith with a stiff clean shirt on. Soon after his arrival on the street, several others in the settlement were seen preparing to go somewhere. About 1 o'clock started for Post Lynne. Will some poor fellow took a ride, representative of the dock to appear upon the left at the last.

E. C. Wiley was doing the sights at Morehead last week. Eh, we the lady customers are so nice.

John Elliott talks of going to Kansas in the spring. Better not.

There was a Social hop at town W——'s last Thursday night. The most of some of the boys it must have been late when they got home and the drivers were——

If "Dead Beat" will come to town we will exchange cards and begin our quill, if he wants it. We advise him not to infringe upon some of his good in a manner too Fool" any more, or he might have some of his good in a manner too pleasant to receive. We think the of the mistake in the heading. There is because he means in one direction, as often that he has which one of the boys he is——

Cheap Mone

We will loan money on Improved Real Estate at 6 p and allow payment to be m installments. E. P. Wh Harrisonvil

PLEASANT VALLEY

Thomas Crooks is digging well.

Frank Clarey, the famous sto per, shipped a car load of hogs.

Joseph Miller returned from where he has taken several clai will go back in the spring.

J. A. Loveridge and nephew Memphis on the excursion an having had a good time.

David, do you want someth your Morrish's cake?

Oh, Will, do you want to t another mule? X Cross Ba

Hoover & Maisey will mak 6 per cent. interest and sm sions, any size; 8 per cent. s on commissions on $1,000 an

♦ 14 ♦

Arthur Brown Registration Certificate
Oct 22, 1948 Smith Dist Alluwe, NO2
References: Jack Inman and EJ Williams

SKETCH

Msbev remembers the
Summer of 1966

A 15 pound baby?

T he year was 1966 and our family was living in Tulsa, Oklahoma. Our family consisted of Max, me and our 2 year old son, Max Jr.

The heat had been intense since early spring and it seemed it would continue for months. We were living in a duplex in 2700 hundred block of East Haskell Street in Tulsa. I believe the actual address was 2707 East Haskell St. It was on the north side of the street.

The duplex was not divided as most duplexes. It was divided into front and back. We rented the back portion. Both units had a kitchen, bathroom and a bedroom. The house had been very nice at one time, I am sure. By the time we rented it the beauty had faded. The kitchen floor boards were sort of "squishy". There were little ants we could not banish. These even had wings. Realized later the pesky things were termites. And, this 20 year old mother tried to sweep them up with a broom!

There was an air conditioner in the window which made a welcome hum as the temperature climbed each day into the triple digits, as the weatherman liked to say. Perhaps he thought it sounded not quite so hot!

The heat was taking its toll on me as I was expecting our second baby in mid-summer, July to be exact.

We had one vehicle, a Ford pickup, which started most of the time.

Max worked second shift. I remember the night he was hurt at work. We could not afford a telephone, so another employee of Okla Steel Castings came to the door, knocking hesitantly. It was difficult to find our front door as it was on the BACK of the house. {Remember we rented the back ½ of the house} He told me Max had been taken to the hospital as he had hit his hand with a large hammer. He said Max was asleep from anesthesia and would not wake for hours.

First thing the next morning, I gathered up the 2 yr. old toddler, found a day care that would take a drop-in, and began to start the pickup. I counted 17 times before it started. But it did start and I found the hospital.

Max had hit his hand all right. I was told that when he hit his finger he washed his finger immediately. In so doing, he evidently washed some of the bone particles down the drain. He was in the hospital for two or three days. He was discharged with his hand bandaged as if it had a boxing glove on it. He was cautioned to be very careful and not get it dirty at all. There was possibility of losing a finger or hand if it became infected.

He recovered and was left with a forefinger h would require another surgery. The final outcome was a finger which was skin stretched over many, many feet of wire. It would never bend again. He compensated and has never complained about the inconvenience or the pain that finger caused. Many people never noticed the stiff finger.

All of this is to say that was a summer to remember. Max's accident, the incredible heat, a baby due in midst of the "happenings". I am sure my parents wondered how we would ever survive all this.

Our two year old was doing well. He was born in 1964 while we were in Sallisaw. He developed breathing problems when a day old; and had to be transferred to a hospital in Fort Smith. The diagnosis was pneumonia. The hospital had no ambulance. Our car had been wrecked just a few days before. It was drivable but the hood was tied down with baling wire. The hood "waved hello" to every car we met on the highway. What would we do? I was sick and could hardly get out of the bed. I could not leave the hospital. There was a couple in the area from our home town. Matter of fact, Max worked with him. His wife was a tiny little woman, beautiful as well.

We asked and Marlene said "sure she would go with Max to take the baby to the hospital in Fort Smith, Arkansas." She told me later she never knew what a ride she was going to take! She said, "Max knew only that his son was 3 days old, critically ill, and he had to get him to another hospital as quick as he could." I could only "groan". She smiled and said "That hood flopped up and down. I just knew it was going to come off. He did not let his foot off the gas. We were going very, very, fast. We went under an overpass and saw a law officer parked at the side. He never even tried to catch us. Just watched. Max never slowed until we got into Fort Smith.". She held the baby in a bassinet in her arms from Sallisaw until they reached Fort Smith Hospital.

Max went and stayed on a couch, or chairs, or the hall way the entire week Max Jr was in there. He would not leave his new born son.

In 1964. I weighed 13 pounds less when the baby was born than when I became pregnant. I was sick for months before the birth; and then contracted child bed fever while in the hospital.

The doctor had told us he could not hear a heartbeat, he was very fearful the baby would not survive. IF it did, he thought it would be a very tiny girl. Everyone was surprised when the baby was an 8 # 12 oz. boy!

When I was to leave the hospital, Dad brought Mother to stay with me a few days. The baby was still in Arkansas but would come home in a few days. I could hardly get out of bed as I was so weak. Mother came and Max's mother came a few days.

So, 2 years later, my Mother and dad were particularly concerned about this pregnancy.

This dr. {in 1966} said the first baby was just larger than I could have very easily and that accounted for a lot of the problems at birth.

This pregnancy, in 1966, had been easier, and the doctor said he would induce labor and not let the baby get as large . . . be easier on me and the baby. I believed him. Evidently, mother was not so sure. The date was set for July 15. The delivery was a dream compared to the first. Another boy and he weighed in at 7 # 15 oz.

Lest anyone think Max Sr. was any less thrilled over son #2 let me tell you another event. Max Sr was always interested in "electronic gadgets". In those days, that meant a radio or a camera or a calculator. We had so little money. We both wanted a camera. We looked in the stores, but I knew they were just beyond our budget. He knew it; but was determined to have a new camera. We had been looking at Sears Store at the Polaroid cameras. Those cameras developed the film. They were "instant" photos. What a grand idea! The film came in picture size cards; after the picture was taken; a person used a sponge and a solution in a pre-moistened vial to coat the photo. I just did not encourage the purchase.

After Justin was born; Max left to go to work. He came back as soon as his shift was over. He had made only one extra stop. He had stopped at Sears and purchased that camera we had been considering. He waited until I was in the hospital and bought the camera! I knew he was so excited about having 2 sons. I only smiled because I knew he had opened a charge account and we would be paying for that camera for a while. That was our life. Few of those pictures remain as one of the "drawbacks" to the instant polaroid prints was they would fade greatly as time passed, even with the solution coating them.

I went home after a couple of days and could not believe how good I felt.

As we had a phone installed just before the baby was born, I called mother when I arrived home. I knew her voice sounded surprised when she realized it was me who was calling.

"Betty? Where are you?"

I told her "Well, I just got home. We stopped at the drug store on the way. Sure good to be home."

"HOME! HOME!" "Why in the world are you home?" I could hear the agitation in her voice.

I was the one who was surprised. "Where else would I be? We stopped at the drug store but, other than that, we came straight home from the hospital"

"But, I thought you would have to stay in the hospital at least a week or two" she said.

"Where did you get that idea?

"YOU just had a 15 pound baby! You need to be in the hospital!" She sounded frantic.

It was my turn to sound surprised. "Where did you get the idea I had a 15 pound baby?" I asked.

Max called and told us the baby was born. He told me on the phone. He said the baby weighed 15 pounds."

I thought just a moment and began to laugh. I realized what had happened. Max always had a low voice. Mother had not heard everything he said. "Mother, the baby weighed 7 pounds and 15 OUNCES . . . . NOT 15 pounds"

There were several seconds of silence. She said, "You, didn't have a 15 pound baby?"

"No, I am home and doing great."

"Well, that's good" she said.

She talked just a few moments and said she had to make some phone calls. I asked her who she was going to call.

"Well, when I was told you had a 15 pound baby, I phoned some friends. Now I have to call them back and set it right!"

I didn't even chuckle, but I wanted to! Bless her heart. Mother knew her fears had become fact when her daughter gave birth to a 15 pound baby!

As our conversation ended, I could hear her saying, "Why I have to call, Ina, Dora, Incie, etc."

The summer of 1966 was hot and filled with life altering experiences. The heat? Well, there came a brief shower which cooled the parched ground. The temperatures did not near the triple digits after the baby was born. It was cooler the rest of the summer.

The summer of 1966 is only a memory today. Max continued working and made a wonderful living for us all the remainder years. There have been many summers since 1966 and God has provided so marvelously in each of them.

How did we manage in those early years? We never lived close to our parents; there was no one to baby sit. We depended on each other and God. I wish God had been our main support in those early years; but that came later. Thank goodness God has been patient.

I am reminded of something I read recently. A coincidence is a miracle when God remains anonymous. I feel the summer of 1966 was full of miracles; from a finger which was not lost to a healthy baby to a pickup with a bad starter. A pickup that started when IIHAD to have it to get to the hospital. And not least was the welcome cooler weather which seemed straight from heaven's portals.

I think of the many summers with heat which threatened to suffocate us. The years before we married were years without even a fan as there was no electricity. The air even had a different smell.

The summers with an evaporative cooler. We were cool all right . . . and damp!

We have had central heat and air conditioning for years. Never, never, do I take it for granted. I am thankful for the memories of those early years. Without the memories of yesterday; I might think it has never been this hot before!

Perhaps I should add another bit here. The company paid Max a "settlement" for the loss of that forefinger. He received $500.00. We wanted to use it wisely. We used the $500 to make a down payment on our first home that year, 1966. It was at 6255 East Marshall Street in Tulsa, OK. Our budget was so tight; my parents were disappointed when we purchased the house. They just KNEW we would not be able to continue having the telephone. They would not be able to get in touch with us or hear their grandson's voices. We DID keep the telephone.

We moved to Broken Arrow in 1970. Max was working at Braden Industries in broken Arrow. He liked working there. There was a "draw back". This was basically a farming community. Many of the men who worked there had summer crops they needed to work. A union contract would come up for approval every 3 years. The contract would come up for a voted; be rejected and Max was out of work. I went to work in Tulsa for a Temporary Employment Agency, Office Overload, and at the tag office in Broken Arrow.

During one of those summers of being out of work due to being "on strike", Max applied at Gardner Denver, a relatively new to the area company in the Industrial District near Pryor. He did not get hired. But, after several months and several phone calls from the company, an agreement was reached and he went to work for Gardner Denver.

We stayed in Broken Arrow with Max commuting to Pryor until our house was sold. We liked Broken Arrow, but felt this was what we needed to do.

He commuted from November of 1974 until May of 1975. Our house sold, school was out and we moved to Pryor into an apartment. We found a house that was being built and we moved into it in October, 1975. I still live in that house today.

I always felt that Max gave up part of himself in order to provide a home for us. We have moved more than once, but have been "homeowners" ever since. A home that I now live in alone. But a home he provided for me. nevertheless.

We rented when Justin was born Max Jr and baby Justin Sept 1966 See the French Door. The other Side was a tiny Living room. We Purchased our First home and Moved from here in the Autumn of 1966

There are no Pictures of the infamous kitchen Ants"

Max Jr and baby Justin 1966

Do You Think They Could Know?

Once there was a tall man
With eyes of steel blue,
He threw a long shadow
And his voice was loud,
But his enemies were few.

His sisters called him "Jum
It was short for Jumbo, don't you see?
I called him "Dad",
'Cause that's what he was to me.
His companion was a little Irish woman,
A quiet soul who hardly uttered a word,
Her will was strong
Her pride was deep, This gray haired
lady who didn't speak.

Even though her name was Frankie
Her sister called her "Toots",
She was teasing as only sisters can do.
But, to the end of her days, her eyes
would light-when she would hear . . . .
"Hi, Aunt Toots, been thinking of you!"
I called her "Mother"
'Cause she was mine.

Times grew hard
But I didn't know,
They worked and worked from dawn to dusk
Wonder if they know, do you think they could?
That, now, I know for what they stood.

Right was right
Wrong was wrong.
Together they fought the fight
For their children's sake, 2 boys and a girl.
Wonder if they know, do you think they could?
That, now, I know for what they stood.

Life brought two grandsons.
They watched the little ones' every move
They heard their every word,
The mention of their names—the very sound
Would bring a smile to the lips
And a light to the eyes
Of Grandpa and Granny Brown

Now it was time to go ahead.
The years of work had taken their toll
Each day he grew more weary
Each day he knew he neared the end.
But no one would he tell this he could not do.

The quiet little woman was left alone.
More still than ever before
Were the rooms of her little home
When he went
So went part of her
Each day she grew more weary

Each day she knew she neared the end
But no one would she tell this she could not do.
Wonder if she knows; do you think she could?
That, now, I know for what she stood.

Lord God Upon High,
I pray your blessings Upon these people
You know them better than I
You saw their hearts full of fear
When I heard their voice so strong
You saw their hearts filled with sadness
When I felt only disapproval,
You saw their hearts full of goodness
When man saw them at home many a Sunday morn.

Why do I wonder?
What do I wish?
Well, it's like this
They have both gone through the Valley
of the Shadow of Death

And, never, no never did I tell them
That now I know
Now I understand
Lord God, do you think
They could know . . . .
Oh, do you think they could?
That now, I know for what they stood.

Msbev in honor of mother and dad
Arthur and Frankie Casey Brown

It is "just a dog"

That is what people say. "He is just a dog. My earliest memory is when I was traded for a tank of gasoline; and gasoline cost .23 a gallon! I mean, there we were, all three of us with our mother. Life was about as near perfect as a little fellow could imagine. I had everything I needed. Of course, when you weigh about 2 ½ pounds, a fellow doesn't need much.

My mother and brother and sisters lived with a fellow who didn't like to stay put in one place very much. At least seemed that way to me. I had known him all my life, all 6 weeks of it.

Mr. Man was driving his car and had placed all of us in the back seat. Mama made sure we were all comfy in the box we were calling home. Mr. Man drove a long time before he stopped at a gasoline station. I didn't know that is what it was called. I had seen him stop before and each time he counted pieces of paper out of his wallet. That wallet seemed to be getting thinner each time we stopped.

Mr. Man kept looking into the back seat of the car. He was talking to the owner of the gasoline station. Mr. Man sure seemed to be proud of us! He kept looking and motioning with his hand toward mama and us kids.

Here comes Mr. Man. We are ready to go. What in the world? The other man is coming over, too. You know, the man who put the gasoline in the car. He looked us over, and told Mr. Man "I guess that would be okay".

"You can have your pick of the bunch" I heard Mr. Man say. What does he mean "have your pick of the bunch?

"I'll take that little reddish fawn colored little one in the corner" the other man said.

This cannot be happening I tried to say. But only little yips came from my throat. I looked desperately at mama. She just looked at me as if to say "This is how it happens, little one, every time, this is how it happens" The man reached down and lifted me up. He was real careful as if he thought I might break. I thought I might break, as well. I closed my eyes because I thought I might be sick. He thought I might be sick, too; so he wrapped me in a towel and placed me in a box on the floor.

"Not sure this one is going to make it. Just felt sorry for the poor guy" he mumbled to himself. "Maybe someone will come in and take this little guy home. He is going to be a cute little dog . . . but, my wife is not going to like it if I take this one home."

The Man left about dark. He left me in the station and told me to sleep well. Ha! I thought how would you sleep if you had just been taken away from your mama and brothers and sisters never to see them again? How well would you sleep?

Finally, I was so weary and my eyes so swollen from tears that I couldn't cry. I did go to sleep. I didn't wake up until the man was unlocking the front door of the station. "Well, little fellow, you look better than you did last evening. Hope you feel better. Let me see if you want to eat some of this food I brought for you."

I did eat and I did feel better. I was still sad and thought perhaps I would just run out the door when the man wasn't looking. Where would I go? I had no idea where I was. I better stay and see what happens, I decided.

"Well, there is Art" the man said as a green pickup pulled into the station.

"Hey, Art," the man hollered. "Come see what I have in here. I think you may be interested."

Art came to the door. I didn't know how he would get into the room . . . the guy was that tall, if not that wide. Art came into the room and looked into my box. "Well, what in the world you got in that box?" said Art.

I thought Art must be a brick shy of a full load if he didn't know what was in the box and he was looking right at me.

"Guy came through here and didn't have any money, completely out of fuel. I traded him some gasoline for this little bitty pup. He looks better this morning, last night I wasn't so sure. I can't take this dog home. Wife already said so. Need to get rid of it before my daughter sees it. I'll make you a real good deal if you would take it."

The gas station man was sure wanting Art to take me to his house. I just wanted to see mama and the others, I tried to hide but there wasn't any place to hide in the box. Abe reached down and picked me up. His hand was so big I just fit right into it. For a big man with a loud voice, he sure had a soft spot for little pups. I could tell without words being said. Found myself hoping Art would take me home with him.

That girl of yours would sure like this little fellow" said the gas station man.

Yeah, and my wife would sure hit the ceiling. This pup is so little, it has got to stay inside. The hawks would pick him up if he stayed outside; they got some chickens last week. Those chickens were a lot bigger than this little runt" said Art.

Somehow I didn't get mad when he called me runt. I knew I could trust Art. Ohh, Pleeeeease take me home, I wanted to say. "What do you want for him?" said Art. "Just pay me what I gave that fellow in gasoline and he is yours" said the gas station man.

"How about I give you $5.00?" said Art. "He is yours. Just take him quick, before my girl decides to come over here and sees him," said the gas station man.

I never knew my daddy. My mama was a tiny little mama. She said our daddy was larger than her just a bit. I looked a lot like mama. I would never be very big, she had told me. My hair was short and sort of reddish brown. My ears were pointed and stood straight out. My eyes . . . well, how do you describe my eyes? They were big and brown and sad. Sad because I was a 2 ½ pound Chihuahua that had been traded for some gasoline and I was on my way to meet some girl who would probably put ribbons around my neck and dress me like a doll. Ohhh, Art tell me that won't happen!"

ART

I put the pup back in the box and put the pup and the box on the seat of the green pickup. I knew I would be home in less than 10 minutes.

The air was blowing in the window; felt good. Then I noticed the pup shivering. I reached over and pulled the towel closer around the runt. I didn't know that this pup would last long. Sure did not want to take it home and Betty get attached to it just to lose it. Had a soft spot for that girl.

I picked the runt up out of the box and took the towel off. The pup just fit into my hand. I opened the door and looked at Betty sitting there. I knew she dreamed a lot. She turned and looked at me.

"Betty, look what I got here." Betty took that runt pup in both of her hands and hugged it so close. The pup liked to be hugged. I knew the pup liked her and Betty liked the pup.

Now, the hard part. I thought I knew what Toots would say.

Just as I feared!

Toots took one look and said, 'What do you have there? Well, that thing is so little, it will have to stay in the house. You sure it is a dog? What in the world are you thinking?"

It was done. Betty liked the runt. She didn't have any little friends to play with; maybe this pup would help.

Toots allowed as how this is just what she needed. I ignored it. Getting off easy I thought.

That little runt pup looked as though he knew she was not happy.

DUPPY JEAN

I heard them talking about house breaking. I figured this house was little, but surely it wouldn't break. Ms. Art went outside but returned shortly. She had a big flat piece of metal, it was enamel coated. Heard her say she got it from the junk pile, it had been a liner in the old stove they had junked. She had that big flat pan and she had put dirt from the garden on that pan.

"I never house broke a dog before" she said. "Surely he isn't so stupid but what he will know what to do in this dirt". Ms. Art put the enamel pan on the linoleum behind the chair Art sat in. I think I heard her mumble something about he deserved to have to be near this mess. Didn't rightly know what Ms. Art meant.

I looked at that pan and thought about it. Betty and Ms. Art finally went into the other room. I could hear their voices, but couldn't figure what they were talking about. Ahh well, I figured I had other business to tend to. More I thought about it, the more I knew I really did have business to tend. I looked at the door and knew I had no way of opening it. I looked at that pan of dirt. I sure did miss being outside. Surely it wouldn't hurt to just put one paw into that cool dirt. I very carefully went over to the pan and put one front paw into the dirt. It felt so good! Ohh, it won't hurt to just stand in it. Soon, I was standing in that nice cool dirt.

Ms. Art sure was nice and thoughtful to bring this pan of dirt in the house, I thought. I sniffed and I could smell the outdoors. Ohh, this was so neat. Before long I was moving that dirt around on that pan. The dirt wasn't very deep and the pan was even cooler under the dirt. Uhhm, must be raining outside. I could hear the splat, splat, splat of big rain drops. I could see out the window and the sun was shining, but I could still hear the splat, splat of the rain. Faster and faster I moved the dirt. Faster and faster it rained. What fun! I had more fun than I had ever had in my 6 weeks of life! Move the dirt, hear the rain drops.

I looked into the other room. I saw Betty look at me. She was moving her lips, but no words were coming out. Strange little girl. I thought she was perfectly normal earlier. Her eyes were big and round, her lips were moving with no words. Even stranger, her one arm was pointing toward me . . . and the other was motioning to her mother. "Ohhhhh, look" Betty finally breathed out loud.

When I quit moving the dirt, the rain drops stopped going splat. I realized that wasn't rain drops hitting the roof. It was dirt hitting the wall, hitting the window, hitting everywhere. I realized I was making that noise about the same time I saw Ms Art come to the door way.

Let me say it this way. On a list of good days that day would not be on it.

Ms. Art came carrying a broom. She picked up the pan of dirt and threw it out the door. She used the broom trying to sweep up the dirt I had . . . uhhh . . . . moved a bit. She tried to reach me with the broom, but I was little and I moved faster than the broom. I ran under the chair. She ran to the chair. I ran to the corner. She ran to the corner. "I knew it! I knew it! I knew it!" "I don't how care how hot or how cold it is outside. This dog will HAVE to go outside! Get that dog out of here" she yelled.

I looked at Betty. She looked at me and I ran to her. She took me to the kitchen and opened the door. Free! Betty told me to stay close. I knew to hide. Whew, safe at last. Uhh ohh. I just thought I was safe. That is a BIG tom cat and he is coming straight toward me. I bet his name is Brutus . . . Ohh, Good Grief, what next.

"Tom, you leave Duppy alone" Betty hollered from the kitchen door. Tom looked at Betty and then at me. I could see he was weighing the consequences very carefully. Tom put his cat nose in the air and walked on down the path. Somehow I knew my life and Tom's life would be veery interesting. Little did I know the adventures which lay ahead of us! But right now, this was home and I was glad.

Post story The end of the story

Duppy Jean (my middle name was Jean and now the dog shared my name) gave us lots of laughs and tears. Duppy Jean was a girl dog. Why we always referred to Duppy as "him" I cannot explain. Probably a trick mother "played" on Duppy! Lazy summer afternoons, we would look out the window into the yard and see the two of them. Duppy asleep curled up against the big tom cat. Both were sleeping soundly next to each other.

While we were living in the shotgun house Duppy and Tom made a lasting impression in our house. One afternoon mother was standing at the kitchen stove when Duppy came to be let in the door. Mother did not even look, but reached over and opened the screen just enough for Duppy to come through. She never noticed what was in his mouth. I saw and was horrified! The little dog pranced by me as though he was a king. There was a mouse in his mouth! It was awful. The dog pranced through two rooms and went into the living room where dad was taking his Saturday afternoon nap. He was snoring away in that navy blue platform rocker. Ohh no! I stayed back. Mother was right behind Duppy. She was talking. Duppy wasn't listening. Duppy looked at mother and growled. Mother stayed back.

Duppy looked at dad, looked around and made his decision. He never put the mouse down. He jumped up onto dad's shoe. Slowly but surely Duppy made his way up dad's leg and on to his chest. Dad was still asleep. He did not know he had a dog with a mouse just inches from his face.

Mother said "Os" 1 (her nickname for dad). If mother would have not laughed so much she would have more success waking dad. I held my breath.

After a few minutes, Dad finally moved his head to the side. Duppy stood patiently. Finally, Duppy began to growl softly as though trying to awaken dad. Dad realized he heard a growl at same time he heard mother's voice. He opened his eyes to see a mouse swinging in front of his nose and hearing Duppy's low growl. Would you believe this? Dad took all this in and immediately said "Good Duppy. Been hunting?" Dad bragged on the little dog and Duppy turned and made his way down dad's leg and jumped off and pranced outside. To the end of her days, mother claimed Tom, her old tom cat, killed that mouse and let Duppy have it!

Duppy had to stay at home when I married. Aunt Lula made the comment "Jum finally had to admit whose dog that is."

One day a couple came to visit in the late afternoon. Mother and dad and the other two people were in the tiny living room. The 6 PM news was on. Usually she turned the tv off when company came. For some reason she had not this day. Suddenly, without warning, mother Jumped up from her chair and ran to the tv.

She had reacted from habit forgetting they had company. She was reminded when she saw the look on the other people's faces. Blushing, mother explained "when the news is on, we watch and turn the volume down when the commercial comes on. You see, one evening someone gave Duppy a piece of candy corn when the Doublemint chewing gum commercial was on the tv. You remember "double the flavor double the fun"? Well, Duppy remembered the commercial after hearing it once! Duppy would jump up and prance over to the candy bowl and stand and yip until he got his candy. Mother explained she had run out of candy corn and didn't want Duppy to hear the commercial until she went to town and got more candy corn.

The years passed. When Duppy became sick and could not get well, Mother and Dad took Duppy to Vinita to a veterinarian each week and then every other day for a pain shot. Dad just could not put the little thing to sleep. Mother told me that one day as they were driving home from taking Duppy to the vet, Dad looked at the dog laying in the shoe box between them on the car seat and said, "Toots, don't ever tell anyone what we are doing." Mother nodded. She never admitted she had become fond of that dog.

In their hour of grief they drove to Vinita to the vet. Could one reason be that it was a lot less likely to see anyone they knew if they drove to Vinita and not Nowata. Self-respecting country folks did not keep little bitty dogs inside the house; much less travel many miles to provide pain control for him.

Duppy died peacefully and was buried on the side of the hill where he chased the old tom cat and the old tom cat chased him.

SKETCH

The Year was 1958

A Politician Came to visit . . . .

We lived in a shotgun house

Beverly Brown Hart

I remember he was tall. He seemed so much taller than mother. Dad stood 6 ft 4 inches tall. Mother stood 5 ft. 4 inches.

His thumb on one hand was "different". The end was round; the nail thick. Childhood accident he said. His cousin dared him to put his thumb on the wood pile; she would chop it off. He did . . . and she did.

Dad remembered his mother picking him up and running with him to a team and buggy. Ma didn't know who owned the buggy. She jumped in with her son and went as fast as she could to town. Dr couldn't do anything. The thumb was attached by skin and nothing else. Ma and pa told the doctor if he couldn't do any better than that, they would just take the boy home. His mom and dad did just that. They took him home. Then, they buried the end of dad's thumb.

Dad would tell people that part of him was already "buried"; particularly after the Oologah Dam was built and "Old Alluwe" was under water! I can still see him grin and say "part of him" was already under that lake!

This story is one of my earliest memories. I realized, when I was grown, he had never told which cousin! Made no difference to him. He made sure it made no difference to me. Forgiving was something he did very well. The year was 1958 and it was so hot. We had electricity now, so we did have an oscillating fan. Afternoons were so hot even the dogs and cats shared the shade of the oak tree. Dad would go early in the morning to cut brush. There was a little church at one corner of the 40 acre pasture. He would park the tractor when he saw cars arriving at church. He tried to NEVER create noise during church service. Part of his "unwritten code of honor".

He rolled his cigarettes with Prince Albert tobacco. He would hold his hand away from him; and shaking his head in "disgust" . . . saying "Betty, just think how much money I would have if I had never begun using this stuff . . . ." I remember dad getting his smithy tools and putting them under the shade of a big tree. Soon, he came leading a horse. The horse decided to "rare back" with his front hooves pawing the air above dad's head. Dad never flinched; just stood his ground.

Being a brave soul and concerned for my dad, I hid behind a tree. Finally, I looked around the tree! Dad was just fine and the horse was getting shod!

I was dreading school in the heat. But being bored I figured being bored at school would be better than bored at home. I was also apprehensive as I thought I might be going to a different school that fall. I had heard mother and dad talking about it a bit.

Then one day, Mr. Politician came to visit.

It was Saturday afternoon and dad had fallen asleep in his chair. His chair being a dark blue platform rocker covered in the cut velvet of that era. The chair had conformed to my dad's frame. When dad fell asleep his head almost touched the wall on the south side of the room. His shoes were only a few feet from the north side of the room. Being a shotgun house*, the pasture to the north and the yard to the south were as near as the window and door of that one room. Some folks had wall to wall rugs, we had wall to wall "dad".

Then the politician came to visit. Mr. Politician was also the Superintendent of school the folks were thinking about sending me. The school I attended did not go past the eighth grade.

The fella entered our shotgun house. He could not miss the worn linoleum. The only breeze stirring the air came through the screen door. Things went just real smooth; til the politician made a slight mistake.

The politician was really a nice guy. I could tell he and dad enjoyed visiting. Then the poor fella did it! He did The "Unthinkable"!

He told dad he could get free lunches for his girl at school. He could get around that $5.00 each month. He sat back, smiling expansively, figuring he had a couple of solid votes for next election. He had evidently not noticed my dad's unusual silence. I had noticed, and I waited. I knew not to smile.

Sitting quietly till now, dad sat straight up as though a board was against his back. He looked at Mr. Politician, and said "I have me a job and I can pay for my girl's lunches. What's more, even if I didn't have me a job, I would pay for my girl's lunches." With each word, his voice became louder, yet somehow he never yelled. When he stopped, he looked at Mr. Politician with a gaze which dared him to misunderstand.

Startled, Mr. Politician wiped beads of perspiration from his forehead as he said "Why, yes sir, I understand. You bet, you can pay for her lunch. Why yes sir, of course. Wouldn't have it any other way. I know you can pay for her lunch. That was . . . uhhhh . . . just a thought. Uhmmm, yessirree just a thought."

Dad and the politician became good friends. Somehow I don't think either ever forgot that afternoon in 1958.

I didn't forget it and I knew that I would never have to wash dishes at the new school; even if dad was laid off again. He was and I never did . . . . It would not have hurt me in the least; but you see; it would have hurt my dad. Too many sad memories for him; he was determined his daughter would never have those memories of doing without.

That is the way I remember the day the politician came to visit us when we lived in the shotgun house in 1958.

Endnote: A shotgun house is one room wide {often 12 ft} and 3, 4, or 5 rooms in length. If you stood in door way of the end room, fired a shotgun, the shot would go through every room in the house without hitting a wall. Hence, a "shotgun house". Our shotgun house had 3 rooms and an added lean-to room which was my bedroom. Popular in the south after the Civil War; the shotgun style remained a common type of house for country people well into the twentieth century. To be honest, I would have described our home as a "poor man's" home; plain and simple

I am pleased to note that Mr. Politician continued to stop by to visit Dad often. He was always welcome, :)

SKETCH

The Year was 1961 ~
It was a Runaway Tractor?

The lad on the tractor . . .
was he a patriot or a prodigal . . .
or was he both?

I remember my mother as she walked across the floor, brushing her hands softly across the front of her apron as she walked into the kitchen.

Not a hint of a smile touched her lips as she began speaking. "You were out late last evening." She said it as a statement; not a question.

I knew mother was right. I was 15 years old and bored out of my mind. I knew this was not going "to be pretty". I told her we had come straight home from town. Did she believe me? I waited for her to continue. She seemed preoccupied.

Mother walked into the kitchen. I could see she was choosing her words with care.

She began talking. "I can remember another day like this one, years ago. Seems like only yesterday your dad came with quite a story to tell. The day was warm for the first week of April. Your dad had left early for the field. I thought it was time he was home."

Of the things I had thought she would say; this was not what I expected. Perhaps I was going to get by easier than I had feared.

Mother continued. "I had sent coffee for the pot your dad kept in the shack at the fields. That gray enamel pot had served him well for quite some time. He said it saved him a trip back to the house. He could just let the team rest while he had his mid-morning coffee. Said those horses got tired like a man got tired."

I had seen that old coffee pot. It had a piece of baling wire holding the lid in place. The hinge had broken long ago. Mother was silent. I wondered if she would continue talking or continue thinking. I mentally voted for the talking. Felt I would fare better the less she thought.

She said, "He did come in with the team and wagon. I knew when he came to the house his mind was elsewhere. "Your dad said "Beats anything I ever saw."

Mother looked at me as if waiting for me to speak. I said, "What was he talking about?"

Your dad asked me "Do you remember we heard about a family moved in over across the river? Someone said they came from

Arkansas. Him and her look way too young to have a house full of kids."

"He had been visiting?" I said.

A slight smile seemed to touch her lips. I must have imagined it. Mother rarely smiled. "No, he had not been visiting. He was driving the team and wagon down the road heading for home; when he saw a runaway tractor."

"A runaway tractor?" I gasped. I had never heard this before.

"Well, that is what he thought it was. Not very many folks had tractors."

"Uhmm," she wrinkled her brow as she tried to remember the year. "You were just a toddler so it must have been about 1948 or so. A few farmers had tractors, but many still used the team and wagon. Your dad was using the team. He was going down the road and up ahead he saw the tractor coming down a slight hill and it was headed straight for the fence and the road just beyond. Knowing there was a large, deep pond just across the road, your dad urged the team on as fast as he dared. Keeping his eye on the run away tractor, he noticed something was different."

I thought a runaway tractor was a runaway tractor. But this sounded good to me. As long as her mind was on a runaway tractor of more than 13 years ago it meant she wasn't thinking about me and what time I came home last evening.

Your dad said, "The more I kept my eye on that tractor, I could not figure what was going on. I got the team up even with that tractor. Figured I could jump on the tractor maybe if it slowed enough."

Even at the time, this did not seem an unusual statement. If anyone could manage this, my dad could do it. A blacksmith, he had muscles like few men. "Where was the driver", I asked; realizing I was caught up in this story. So much for playing it "cool"!

"I am getting to that" she said. "Your dad managed to get the team and wagon even with the tractor and the strangest thing happened. That tractor turned sharply before it hit the fence. That is when he realized the tractor did not have a driver. It had two drivers. Two little boys. One was steering the tractor, but he could not see over the wheel. Another boy was standing next to the boy in the driver's seat. The boy standing was giving directions to the one steering! Your dad just sat in the wagon and watched as the two boys went on with their work. He said those little'uns were not big enough to see over that steering wheel, yet they were doing a man's work."

Mother looked at me with those gray eyes that seemed to know more than I dared to imagine.

"Did you decide who the boys were driving the tractor?" I asked.

"Ohh, he knew. Your dad just shook his head and said it was that family who moved in from Arkansas. We only had 3 kids, so your dad thought anyone with 5 kids was a large family. The family did not stay in the river bottom too long. Moved back to Arkansas I heard. I heard they moved into town few years ago. They live north of town, now."

My curiosity was obvious, so I asked her "who was the family?"

Mother looked at me with no emotion showing. Very quietly she said, "You were out with one of those little kids last evening."

Why mother said no more, to this day, I do not know. What was on her mind? Was she thinking back to the years gone by? She was probably remembering 1949 and 1950. So much on their minds during those years.

What would my dad decide to do about his dad? Dad had to make the decision. The "old man" was clearly sick in body and mind. Dad was considering moving the family 25 miles east just so he could be a bit closer to his father; even if all Dad could do was visit the old man. Mother was not fond of the river bottom, but it was all she had known since coming to this land of muddy rivers prone to flooding; and wind that burned your skin in the summer. And the cold that seemed to melt into your bones.

She did not tell her friends back home about her life here. How she would shake the snow from the top of the quilt when she arose in the morning. That house was hardly more than a shack. She was grateful she no longer shook snow from the quilt, but ice still froze on the inside of the windows making the windows appear to be etched by an invisible hand. Those years of 1949, 1950, 1951 had their distinct concerns; but would her only daughter be her biggest challenge? Only time would tell.

Was she wondering if the incident of 13 + years in the past would remain history? Or, would it be woven into the life of our family; just as surely as the threads of a tapestry?

I remember her telling me the story about dad and the runaway tractor. I remember her being lost in thought. Would she relive that incident over the coming years? Did she believe me when I told her I came straight home from town? I never had the courage to ask her. I did not have the courage to ask her many years later. Many years after I had married one of those boys; both of whom grew up to be fine young men.

I am sure mother and dad both wondered if my life would be like that of the Run Away Tractor; seemingly headed for sure tragedy; only to turn at the last moment. As sure as the hot summer of 1960 turned to the cold winter of 1961, our early years of marriage seemed to be on a one way path to destruction. We were self-destructing; but those years were short. The remainder of our years together I was blessed to live with a most intelligent and caring man.

The youngster driving the "run away tractor" remained a bit of a daring man. Our lives were blessed. He never ceased to amaze me.

He was a man of few words. I told him that every day God gave him 500 words to use. After he used those 500 words, he did not ask for any more to use that day. He waited until the next day for his next 500 words. Sometimes I teased him and told him "I'm your interpreter". He never disputed the statement. Probably because he figured it would "count toward his daily ration of 500 words".

I am sure that my husband and I, and our sons, all descendants not yet born, were never far from the hearts and minds of mother and dad the remainder of their lives. The life they lived very near where dad saw his future son-in-law as a small boy on a "run a way Tractor".

Mother used a Brownie camera to take this picture @ 1960

I remember Mother Taking this picture about 1960 or 1961.
She used a Brownie camera.

This picture is probably
5 or 6 years after the
"Run a way tractor" event.

SKETCH

Polly's Hero
Patriot or Prodigal?

I can hardly remember the first time I saw him. He seemed bigger than life, with a laugh that could be heard in the next county. Those who did not know him well would think him another poorly educated part-time farmer, part-time blacksmith, full-time "country bumpkin". But those were the ones who did not know him at all.

Anyone could see the shirt cuffs that would not button, the shoe size 13EEEE. Those had to be ordered from Sears Roebuck catalogue. The shoe store in town sure did not carry that size. I think it was his size that intimidated me . . . . until I got to know him. His family called him "Jum". I asked his wife why. She simply said, "It is short for Jumbo". Not an extra pound upon his frame, just a jumbo man.

When you spoke to him, you noticed the bright blue eyes, which sparkled from a weather-beaten face with a hint of his native American heritage. Not yet 25 years old, he was a striking figure of a man . . . all 6 foot 4 in. You might notice the knuckles in his hands, the bones in his wrists, skin stretched taught, and you knew the strength contained within the man.

His laughter and his strength you would soon recognize. Whether you saw him stand without flinching as a horse reared in front of him, or you heard the booming laugh as he thought of something funny, you knew Jum was what he seemed to be. But, there was more to this man.

The oldest of six children, Jum quit school after the eighth grade. Not much thought went into the decision as his dad was gone for months on end. Fur trapping the old man said.

The old man stood 6' 7" tall. He was a private person. Either his size or his pearl handled revolvers kept most folk at a distance. The old man gave no answers. He simply appeared and then he left.

Someone needed to put food on the table for Ma and the little ones. Even as the hot July sun beat down upon him, Jum kept thinking of the coming winter

Ma, the kids, especially Polly. How could Jum provide for Ma and the kids? He had a "soft spot" for Polly; couldn't bear the thought of her being hungry. One thing for him to be hungry, or even Ma. But not little Polly.

Polly's two older sisters were the prettiest girls in the county. Polly was born with a split lip, and her eyes were "different". It wasn't very noticeable but she still dreaded going to school sometimes.

Even her Father could hardly look at her without saying something to make her cry. The old man was gone so much, Jum sometimes wondered if the old man didn't have another family settled in up the river.

Jum dreaded Christmas! He knew he shouldn't feel that way. Winters were so harsh for Ma and the kids. No Christmas toy for little Polly. He had to figure out something for Polly. He began to form a plan.

It was a long ride into town. If the river was up he would catch the ferry. He sure didn't want to get the saddle wet and muddy. A saddle like this one was hard to come by. Custom-made of leather with silver conchos, Jum had won the saddle fair and square. He guessed that helping Ma chop wood for $1.50 a day had made him stronger than he thought. He hardly had to work up a sweat to win that saddle. Game called Arm Wrestling. Jum called it a "Sure Thing". He hoped his plan worked as well as the Arm Wrestling.

The ride into town would have been real pleasant if he didn't have so much on his mind. He located Attorney Sawyer the first thing. He didn't have too far to look.

Attorney Sawyer liked the big, tall man. Sawyer, like most of the other businessmen in town, had lost most of his savings in the recent "crash". He couldn't imagine what Jum wanted.

Sawyer listened intently as the big man talked. It became apparent that Jum had thought for some time about this plan. Sawyer finally asked Jum if he was sure about this.

Jum simply nodded. Jum loved that saddle, knew he would never have another like it. Sawyer knew it too.

The "plan" was agreed. Sawyer would own the saddle. Jum would receive no money as Sawyer was nearly penniless himself. One thing

Sawyer owned and had almost forgotten about it. It now belonged to Jum.

People knew better than to ask Jum why he was riding bareback. Most probably assumed he had lost the saddle the same way he had acquired it.

Jum's feet were almost dragging the ground as he rode up the dirt road toward the shack where Ma and the kids lived. He heard Polly's shout before he saw her! He hoped Polly would not notice the gunnysack he had thrown across the horse behind him. He handed the gunnysack to Ma. Polly was talking a "mile a minute" and didn't seem to notice the sack.

December came as they knew it would. The winds blew cold against the little shack. Polly rose early Christmas morning, with little thought of presents. Ice coated the inside of the windows, and Polly's breath formed icy fog in front of her face. Ma gave Polly a rare smile.

Ma went to the old trunk in the corner of the kitchen. Lifting the lid, she removed a gunnysack. Polly recognized it! She knew it was the same gunnysack Jum had given to Ma the past summer. Inside was the prettiest doll Polly had ever seen.

As Ma held out the doll to Polly and said, "Merry Christmas, honey" Polly couldn't believe her ears. The doll had once sat on a shelf in Attorney Sawyer's office. A china head atop a muslin body, the doll had belonged to Attorney Sawyer's daughter, long since grown. Now it belonged to Polly, because Jum had a plan. Polly would not forget that Christmas as long as she lived!

Is this story true? That is the question . . . . I am sure

About 30 years ago. Polly told me about receiving the doll that cold Christmas day. She remembered ma getting the doll from the trunk that Christmas morn. She could see (in her memory) so clearly . . . . Jum coming down the dirt road with the gunny sack behind him; and he handing the sack to mama. She knew Jum brought her a Christmas present in hot summer. Polly knew all her life that Jum loved her. Jum was her hero as long as she lived. Polly wanted to tell me the story because she knew that I also knew Jum.

This story is about people who lived in a time which revealed their "trueness". Jum was as real and true as any man could be. Polly was as real and true as any sister could be. I even remember their mother. All her children called her "ma.

How did Jum get the doll? Did he have a saddle? Did he have an agreement with a lawyer in town? Who knows? He knew the lawyers in town. I am reminded of a saying attributed to Will Rogers. "Never trust anyone who can only spell a word one way" As in all real life stories, the true story is the story in your heart.

Ohh yes, Polly's hero was real and she called him Jum. He was real to me; I called him Dad.

The late newsman Tim Russert said that not only did our ancestors shape us . . . we stand on their shoulders.

I do know this may have happened just as it is written. Yes, not only did our ancestors shape us, we do indeed stand on their shoulders.

No. 398

DEPARTMENT OF GAME AND
OKLAHOMA CITY, OKLA.

Date _____ Dec _____ 3 _____ 19__

Name _____ J. W. Brown _____, Town of _Nowata_

County of _Nowata_, State of Oklahoma, b

lawfully in possession of a resident hunting license No. __
for the current year and having paid the annual license fe
$1.25 as required by law, is hereby licensed and author
to trap for fur bearing animals as provided by law,
amateur trappers.

Age _59_ yrs. Weight _175_ lbs. Height _6_ ft XX

Color of eyes _Blue_, Color of hair _Brown_ Race _Whi_

THIS LICENSE EXPIRES JANUARY 31st, 1939
This License Is Not Transferable.

N. D. TURNER
Game and Fish Warden.

Asst. Game and Fish Ward

his license must be carried by the licensee while trapping, in
addition to his or her hunting license for the current year.

The trapping season opens December 1st, 1938, and closes
January 31st, 1939. The following furbearing animals can be
taken: Raccoon, Skunk, Opossum, Muskrat, Badger, Mink and
Civet Cat. Every trapper is required to make a report of all
fur taken within 30 days after the close of the season. The
holder of this license is limited to the use of 10 traps of
four inch spread.

PREDATORY ANIMALS

Wolf, Bob Cat, Coyote and Wild Cat can be taken at any time.

—THIS SEASON IS CLOSED—

on Fox, Beaver, Otter, Sable and Marten. See Sec. 65 and 68
of the 1933-35 Game and Fish Laws

Copy of license in Mother's Picture Album. Wes'Trappers License Front
Side Evidently No To measure height of
This man 6 Ft XXX
Back Side
of Oklahoma Trappers License.

Copy of WWI Registration Card for John Wesley Brown, my grandfather. He states he is working for Robt. Lee at General store in Alluwe

Grandmother Vic tiny 2 room house in Chelsea

family

generations

Lula brought her mom to visit Arthur's family at Vinita

Howard   Grandma (Vic Tilton) Brown   me (Bev Brown Hart)   Lonnie
        Mother (Frankie brown)   Aunt Lula Brown Triplett

Lula brought her mother to visit Jum's family at Vinita, OK
@ 1951

SKETCH

Jum Meets a Lady from Arkansas

J um couldn't concentrate. He wondered if he was "normal". He shouldn't be that nervous about meeting this girl. His mind wandered as he thought about his recent date with Chantelle.

Jum decided he STILL didn't know what made her so persnickety. He had acted like a gentleman, leastways how he thought gentlemen were supposed to act. Not that he had ever seen a "real" gentleman, much less been around one for any length of time. He had arranged it so everything would be perfect when he went to call on Chantelle.

Everyone knew the smithy had the prettiest horse drawn buggy in Smithville. Jum worked for the smithy one week in exchange for the use of the buggy for one afternoon.

Jum had dressed in his best clothes before going to Chantelle's house. She was ready to go when he arrived.

"No, you don't really need to meet my parents," she had said. That really isn't necessary. We modern girls don't go in for that old fashioned stuff anymore."

Jum thought he really should meet her folks. But, Chantelle ought to know. She had fixed a picnic lunch. Jum thought the basket was not like any basket he had ever seen. This one had cloth in it and there were plates and cups and silverware packed in it. And the food! Why, he had never seen so much fried chicken, potato salad, and apple pie! Jum remembered feeling guilty and wishing Ma and the kids could have shared it. He didn't say a word about that to Chantelle. After eating, Chantelle wanted to ride in the buggy. Time sure went quickly. Five hours had passed before he knew it! Chantelle did say she needed to be heading home before too long. He drove up the river to Lightning before turning the buggy east toward Smithville.

As they neared Smithville, Jum thought Chantelle seemed jittery or nervous.

"Chantelle, are you okay?" he finally managed to say.

"Why, yes," Chantelle replied.

"I was just wondering,. You haven't said much the last two or three miles."

"Well to be honest, I really do need to find a rest room pretty soon," she said.

Jum remembered replying, "Whatsa matter? Ya tired?" He would carry the look on her face to his grave. How would he know that was what city folks called an indoor bathroom? He had heard of them, but he had sure never seen one!"

Chantelle told him that the Smithville Chamber of Commerce had a rest room. They were within two blocks of it. Shortly, Jum stopped the buggy and helped Chantelle get out of the buggy.

After Chantelle returned, Jum took her home. He didn't ask her if he could see her again.

And here he was on his way to meet another girl! Jum's cousin, Ben, had just married a girl from Arkansas. Ben's bride had two sisters; the youngest was unmarried and living with Ben.

Jum sort of had the idea her father had sent her to Oklahoma to encourage her to quit seeing someone in Arkansas. He also had heard rumors of fur collars, silk stockings, and patent leather shoes.

He had also heard that Madge's dad had lost almost all his savings in the "Crash". Depression is what politicians were calling it.

Just what he needed, to play second fiddle to someone he had never seen! Jum figured Ben really just wanted him to give him and his bride an afternoon alone. Okay with Jum.

Jum knew it would take a miracle for him be able to support a wife as long as Pa wasn't around. He also knew he couldn't live with himself if he didn't help Ma and the kids.

Before he knew it, he found himself at Ben's house. They were all sitting on the front porch. When he dismounted, he knew immediately which was Madge. Madge had brown wavy hair, big gray eyes and she acted like she wanted nothing to do with him! When she stood up, she didn't even come up to his shoulder. He was 6' 4" and she was at least 12" shorter! Jum did not have the money to rent a fancy buggy to take this lady for a ride. "Would you like to go for a walk?" he finally asked her.

"Sure", she said.

They left the horse in the lot beside the barn and took off toward town. Jum noticed how she had to really work at keeping up with his stride, so he slowed without saying a word. If she noticed, she never mentioned it. Cousin Ben lived in tiny Lightning, so it didn't take long to walk the length of Main Street. "Would you like to walk to the creek?" Jum asked. She sure didn't say much, he thought. Couldn't tell if she was upset or just quiet. Gosh, Jum sure wished he knew more about women!

After walking about thirty minutes, they reached the creek and decided to sit on the grass and rest a bit. Jum couldn't help but think that this girl was different from Chantelle, but every bit the lady. A lady would never want to see Jum again. He couldn't blame her. Might as well enjoy the afternoon, he thought.

"Do you have a family?" Madge asked. Jum thought about lying. But, he had to be honest. "Well, yes, I do. I have a Ma and 6 younger brothers and sisters. I don't live with them. I do help them a lot."

"Is your Pa dead?" she asked. Natural question, Jum thought. "No, he ain't dead. Least if he is, we don't know it. He just isn't around much."

Quietly, Madge said, "You know, a man that will take help take care of his Ma and little brothers and sisters is a True Gentleman." Jum couldn't believe his ears. A lady thought he was a gentleman! He had never been so happy in his life! Just to have Madge by his side as he walked her home. Somehow, he knew this was not the last time he would be seeing Madge. Perhaps Ma was right. God would provide.

Note:

You may be thinking . . . "Well is this tale true or not?" On a rare occasion Mother would tell me a story. One afternoon, she began to smile and chuckle. She told me . . . or rather whispered this little incident.

"You know your Dad did take a lady on a date. He did make the remark which Mother laughed so hard in the telling of this; I thought she would

not be able to breathe! Mother would be about to stop laughing and she would think about dad's remark {what'sa matter? Ya tired?) And Mother was laughing again."

Madge: Mother reminds me of Madge. She did live with her sister and brother in law. The town of Alluwe was near Lightning Creek. Alluwe was first named Lightning before it was named Alluwe.

Needless to say "Chantelle" . . . not her name . . . did not become my mother. "Madge", not her name, did become my mother!

SKETCH

Simply . . . .
Calvin Brown

Calvin Brown:

This is the place; the time; for me to write a few words about you. Dear Great uncle, you have made this just a bit difficult. Do you know that you "disappeared"? You did.

I know you had a brother just about 3 years older than you. His name was John Wesley Brown. He was called "Wes" by most folks. Wes was my grandfather.

One of the things I know about my grandfather is that he was a "loner". Something about him "warned" other people he was not a man you would want to "rile". Probably his size intimidated most. My father said "The old man was quite a bit taller than me. Probably around 6' 7" tall. My dad, Wes' oldest son, was 6' 4" tall. Calvin, from your picture, you were tall as well.

I also have a copy of your marriage license, Calvin. You married Mary Moore in 1905. You gave your address as Kansas, Indian Territory. Mary Moore gave her address as Whitmire, Indian Territory. My husband and I drove to the vicinity of Whitmire just about 3 weeks ago. It is just south of Oaks, OK. Was it "Indian Country" then? It is today and I think it was at that time. As we drove through the area, I could not help but wonder if you had been inside the school, the mission, did you walk those roads? Did you ride your horse from your house to Mary's house? Did you drive a buggy to Tahlequah I T when you went for supplies?

Were you like him, Gr Uncle Calvin? Were you like your brother? Did you do a lot of things together? I know you lived with him for a while. I saw your name on the census for 1910. You were staying with Wes and Victoria and their 3 year old son, Arthur. Arthur became my dad. Gr Uncle Calvin, you no doubt played with your nephew, didn't you? Did you hold him on your lap? Did it bring memories of Mary and what would never be? Did you have to leave, Calvin? Where did you go?

And, Calvin, what happened to Mary? Did she die in child birth? Did she go back to her family when she realized just how difficult her life would be; married to a guy with an untamed spirit within? Lots of questions that will probably never be answered.

You married her in 1905 but you were staying with Wes in 1910; and I find no record of either of you after that.

Calvin, you disappeared. And you intended to do that? Were your killed; or did you choose to change your name and identities? Did you move to another state? So many questions . . . that are really unimportant.

Is it true? You know what Wes told his son {my dad} before he died. Wes told Arthur Brown that the family name used to be Mattix, Maddox, Mattocks (?). We now know Wes was talking about his mother who had married Mr. Mattocks before Andrew Brown. Wes was gone from home a lot. The family was told he was trapping or hunting. Was he with you, Calvin? Or were you in another state? Or were you already gone to "Glory"?

A very precious thing I know, Calvin. Perhaps you did not know it the last time you saw your brother, Wes Brown. The only way I know you even existed is because of Wes.

You see, when Wes knew he needed help in his last days, Arthur came to Wes to make their plans. Wes gave Arthur his treasured possessions, two pictures. One picture was of Wes' sister, Fannie Reay, and the other was of YOU. Calvin, from what I have been told about Wes; his being gone so much. I have been told he lived next to the river; that he traveled by boat a lot. With "varmints" in the house, with rain coming through the roof; these pictures are in remarkable shape. Where did he keep these? I cannot imagine. I have tried to think. Wes lived in a one room shack next to the river some of the time. Did Wes have a tin box? A glass jar?

He protected your picture, Calvin. Wes gave the picture to his son; who gave it to his wife, Frankie. My mother protected your picture,

Calvin. She made sure I knew about you. She wanted me to know about you even though she never knew you!

You were loved, Calvin. You were loved. Rest in peace, Dear Great Uncle Calvin, rest in peace. Questions do not have to be answered. Rest in peace.

Picture which Wes gave to my dad when Wes knew he was ill.
Was this a picture taken when Calvin married?

Beverly Brown Hart

THE PENDULUM OF TIME
"Another observation of 23rd Psalm"

The Pendulum of Time is my master
But my master is not so sure of me.

He tempts me with good thoughts
He leadeth me into Frustration.

He disrupts my thinking;
He leadeth me into paths of confusion
And resentments to keep me occupied.

Yea, though I walk through the
Valley of Good Intentions
I will not act ~ I have become too busy.

He preparest a table before me
In the Midst of distorted priorities;
But, my Lord, the True Master
Sits at the Head of the table.

He quiets my thoughts; sorts my priorities
And tosses aside resentments.
His cup is full of peaceful contentment.

Surely goodness and mercy shall
Follow me all the days of my life
As I dwell in the Protection
Of His Love Forever Amen

                                        bev hart

These Things I Remember about my Dad

He had a sense of humor. I remember dad's sister told me this story. Aunt Pauline loved children. She and her husband, Melvin had 3 boys; Buster, Phillip, Larry. Aunt said she had given birth to her first daughter, Roberta Faye,

Aunt was sitting in a rocking chair in the front room of the house when she heard a truck pull into the drive in front of the house. She looked out the window and knew Jum and Toots had come to visit and see the new baby.

She heard his footsteps come up on the porch but he did not knock on the door. The next thing she heard was the most awful banging on the door and Jum's loud voice "You in there Pauline? I come to DROWN THAT GIRL!"

Aunt Pauline chuckled and said "Your dad knew how proud I was of that girl. I knew what he was doing. He didn't scare me."

I do believe dad had a special place in his heart for his little sister, Pauline. She knew it, too.

I remember dad keeping a white enamel pitcher of water in refrigerator. He drank directly from the pitcher. I remember dad eating all-bran for breakfast every morning.

I remember dad and mother making an order from Sears and Roebuck every fall. I would get new shoes probably. Dad had to order his shoes as he couldn't get them in town. He wore size 13EEEE. Bless her heart, I do not remember mother ever ordering hardly anything. She just did without so much.

I remember mother laughing one day and telling me that she told dad, "Just think how tall you would be if half of you weren't turned under"! No, I do not know how often she told him that . . . . probably not too often

I remember dad taking the tractor to the pasture to brush hog. He would go early in the morning before it got too hot. There was a little church at one corner of the 40 acre pasture. Sometimes dad would come home earlier than he intended. He always watched, and (ESPECIALLY IF IT WERE SUNDAY) he would take the tractor home when he saw cars coming to church. He tried to NEVER create noise during their church service. Part of the "unwritten code of honor of an honorable man".

I remember him taking his grandsons for a ride around "the country mile" in his pickup whenever the grandsons came to visit. Dad would simply drive them around the section. He would be so proud if one of the neighbors saw him taking his grandsons for a ride!

I remember him rolling his cigarettes with Prince Albert tobacco; holding his hand away from him; and shaking his head in "disgust" . . . saying "Betty, just think how much money I would have if I had never began using this stuff . . . ."

I remember dad getting his smithy tools and putting them under the shade of a big tree. Soon, he came leading a horse. The horse decided to "rear back" and delay this "shoeing stuff". Dad never flinched; just stood his ground. I hid behind a tree and just barely looked around the tree! But, dad was just fine and the horse was getting shod!

Brother Lonnie tells me of the time dad was going to go hunting for a squirrel. Dad had not been hunting for a while and did not know where the rifle was kept at the moment. Dad asked for the rifle and two shells. Lonnie went and got the rifle and a box of shells. Dad said "nah, don't need a box of shells. Going after two squirrels, need two shells." I wasn't there, but I can "see" this taking place.

Finally, Lonnie convinced dad to take three shells. Wasn't long before two rifle shots were heard. Here came dad walking down the road. He had two squirrels and handed Lonnie a shell. Lonnie said that rifle shot low and to the left, but dad had remembered and hit the squirrels in the head. This was to not ruin the edible parts of the squirrel.

Dad liked to have a horse on the place. I never was brave enough to ride unless someone else was up on the horse with me. Both Lonnie and Howard would ride.

I remember two horses, Roxie and Cricket. When we lived east of Vinita Lonnie wanted to ride Cricket down the road to his friend's, nicknamed Red, house. There was a bridge close to Red's house. One day as Lonnie was riding Cricket across the bridge, he saw a cottonwood tree down the creek lying on its side. Just as Lonnie and Cricket were riding across the bridge, an old cow got up from behind the tree. The cow had been lying down and chose that moment to raise up and let out an "Oklahoma cow bawl" as it rose. Talk about spooking a horse! Brother said Cricket turned around and headed back where they had been! He tried and tried to get Cricket across that bridge. He went back down the road and started all over but that horse never went across that bridge again. Least not with Lonnie on it!

Dad's middle name was the initial "T". When he was in the CC Camp there were so many men named Arthur Brown, it was confusing. So, the men were given a letter of the alphabet as their middle name. Dad received the initial "T".

Dad called mother "Toots". Mother lived with Faye a while after coming to Oklahoma. She told me her sis, Faye Denton, had given her the nickname. There was a song on the radio and part of the verse was "Toot Toot Tootsie", Sis began calling mother "Toots". It remained her nickname.

Dad also called mother another nickname. If he thought she was going to disagree with him; he might say "You better go ask your mammy." I am not too sure that was a good omen!

SKETCH

Flood Water were a'rising

And the baby was a'coming

Mother told me this story or I would not believe it. I was a teenager. Perhaps she thought I needed to know that sometimes a person just made do with what they had. I do know she thought I spent way too much time wishing and not working!

Mother said the year was 1945, WWII was becoming history. Born before WWI, living through the Depression and WWII, Mother was ready for life to be bit easier.

She said "Seeing as how your two older brothers had been born at home, it just may be time I should go into town and have this baby." She went to the doctor once or twice and plans were made for the delivery. She would go into Nowata for the delivery.

Mother and dad were living at Alluwe, Ok, a small farming community midway between Nowata and Chelsea, OK. My father's family had settled at Alluwe, Indian Territory before 1890, almost 20 years before Oklahoma became a state in 1907.

October came and she knew it wouldn't be too much longer. Her birthday came and . . . went, no baby. Oct 19 was the day, she knew it was time to go to the hospital. Mother made arrangements for her sister to care for the boys, age 6 and 13. Mother and dad started the trip into town. When they got to the Verdigris River they found it roaring at flood stage. The bridge could not be crossed. A flooded angry river was between the hospital and them! I have seen the Verdigris at flood stage, the water churning with debris. What could they do? Mother became quiet. I knew she was remembering that day.

I did not understand. I had been told I had been born in the hospital in town. This was news to me!

Mother said, quietly "Your dad made a raft." Just another task to be done . . . a small delay Yes, a raft upon which he placed my mother who was in the final stages of labor. Mother said "I sat on that raft and thought. ohh good grief this baby is going to be born in the middle of this nasty river"!

They did get to the other side of the river. People had received word of what was happening. The number of telephones in the river bottom community could probably be counted on the fingers of your two hands. That did not keep the news from spreading. Friends and country neighbors gathered to help them. A car was waiting for them. Mother and dad got into the back seat of the car and headed toward town. Only about 4 miles and they would be at the hospital.

The unspeakable happened. That awful knock of a flat tire was loud. What a time to have a flat tire! Mother said it was hard for people to have good tires as it was "war time" and the rubber was needed for the war effort.

Again, word had gone before them. Mother's sister and brother in law had heard that Mother and Dad were on their way in to town. It was only a short time before uncle arrived in his car, picked up mother and dad, and drove them into the hospital at Nowata. I asked mother what the Dr did when they arrived.

Mother just smiled the smallest smile, said "the dr. took my blood pressure, shook his head and waited for the baby." It was a SHORT wait; mother gave birth to a 10 lb. 11 oz. girl. Of course that girl was me!

She said "We never worried about you being "mixed up with the other baby born that day. That little girl only weighed about 2 lbs."

I have wondered why mother did not tell me this story until I was almost grown. Really, I don't think she realized how awesome a lady she was. Just one more short chapter in the life of a woman I knew simply as "mother". Mother was absolutely a Woman of spectacular courage; but she never "had a clue"!

Picture taken in 1946, I was not quite one year old.

We lived east of Vinita, OK on a ranch while my grandfather, John Wesley Brown, was a resident at Eastern State Hospital

After Wes died, my father and mother moved the family back to Nowata County to a house near the Verdigris River at Coodys Bluff

At Vinita I was 5 years old Never did get the "right touch to milk a cow; even this unsuspecting calf.

Beverly "Betty" ca. 1950

Bev milking cow

Beverly on horse with Howard watching over ca. 1949

Lonnie on horse. Pics of Beverly and Lonnie on horseback
taken on highway 60 east of Nowata, west of Verdigris River Bridge.
Evidently little auto traffic!

Lonnie on horse Howard standing

OZARK ANGEL

There is a secret told to me many, many long years ago
A secret just for girls and boys; my mama told me so.
'tis about An Angel like none other,
An angel who's with us wherever we might go.

Are you sometimes sad and lonely
When no friends are around to play?
Or did you try so hard to help; . . . yet no one said
"Job well done, I'm proud of you today!"

Let me tell you mama's secret about an Ozark Angel in the sky,
An Ozark Angel is like none other, mama told me the reason why.
Turn your eyes to heaven, look very closely, and you will know
Beside clouds so white and fluffy an Ozark Angel is always nearby.

Shhh! You must be ever so quiet and there it will be!
The tip of a wing or the edge of a halo is what you will see!
An Ozark Angel is with you no matter how tall you grow
Or if a hundred million miles you go!

Don't forget what I've told you about this Ozark Angel . . . yours and mine.
When skies are dark and troubles come, you mustn't fear it's true!
Just think of our special secret and you will know,
Behind the clouds an OZARK ANGEL is a'watching out for YOU!

By bev In memory of mama
Frankie Casey Brown
Native of "the Ozarks"
Newton County, Arkansas

SKETCH

Casey

The Betty Jean Story

I want to tell you about a little girl named Betty Jean. One summer, something special happened to her. That summer she discovered something about her mama she had never known before. But first, let me tell you where Betty Jean lived. She lived not far from here. She lived near the Verdigris River in a house built before statehood. Today, you could reach the area in little more than an hour. But think about it. There was no electricity. No running water so that meant no TV, no electric iron, no toaster, no microwave, no hair dryer, no indoor bathroom . . . . Their mail box was two miles away on the highway. Betty Jean lived two miles farther than the U S Postal Service could deliver mail! When the rains came, as they always did, she was even more isolated. Even the school bus could not cross the low water bridge. Sometimes weeks went by and the only person Betty Jean saw was her mama or her dad or her brother. She was sometimes very lonely . . . especially as her mama was so quiet. Betty Jean had moped for days 'cause it looked as though

ca. 1949~ Arthur Brown with dau Beverly "Betty Jean"....she is always where her dad is..

there would be no trip to see her Arkansas Aunt and Uncle this summer. It would take most of the day to get there in the old truck, but that didn't matter. Just cause she was eight years old didn't mean she didn't understand. She understood all right. They didn't get to go every year. Surely, Dad and Mother would decide they could pay for the gas for the old red truck.

The dust billowed as Betty Jean danced in the dusty road in front of the house. Mother had just told her, "Get your clothes packed. We will be leaving for Arkansas in just a day or two."

Betty Jean knew to get a couple of changes of clothes for herself, just as her dad, mother, and brother would do. Oldest brother would stay home and look after the place. Anyone knew you couldn't just up and leave the livestock. Someone had to stay behind. The old wooden wagon seat was pulled out of the shed and placed on the bed of the old red truck. It was placed up against the cab. Middle brother would ride back there as usual.

The day finally arrived. Betty Jean had slept very little the night before they were leaving. Before daylight she was up and ready to go. She just decided to go outside and get in the truck. She would just wait on them.

It seemed like a long time, but it probably was not. Brother came out of the house and there was Dad and Mother coming behind. They loaded the truck. Appeared as though her mother had something in her hands. Looked like a large package. Betty Jean wondered just where her mother thought she would put one more thing in that truck. It was going to be a tight fit as it was!

Sure enough, mother had a package. As mother neared the truck, she handed the package to Betty Jean's dad. He took a piece of rope he was carrying and wrapped it around and around that package. When he neared the truck, he wrapped that rope around the outside of the cab of the truck. The package stayed in that spot for the entire trip to aunt and uncle's house in Arkansas.

The old red truck groaned and creaked for might near seven hours. Betty Jean was so tired of being jostled on the rough roads. Her Dad called them "washboard roads".

Only have to ford one more creek and go up the mountain and we will be there" said Dad. Aunt and Uncle lived on the "flat" of the mountain. Betty Jean knew The "Flat" is the top of the mountain before you begin the trip down. She sometimes wondered if the "town kids" knew things like that.

As they drove past a few scattered cabins and houses; Betty Jean could see kids and grown-ups peeking around the edge of broken windowpanes and from behind the corners of the buildings. Her mother told her to stop staring; the people meant no harm. They just knew they were not locals. By the time they arrived at Aunt's house, the neighbors would know strangers were on the mountain.

Mother wasn't saying much but she never did talk much. Was she thinking about how sister raised her after their mama died? Mother said she stayed with her older sister lots of times after mama died. Frankie was such a lonely little girl when her mama died . . . being the youngest and all. Mama told Betty Jean about her mama's beautiful long hair and how pretty her mama was; but she got sick and was in bed for a long, long time. Her papa even took mama to the Mayo Clinic but they could not help Margaret.

Mother always felt so good when, as a little girl, she visited her older sister, Floy, or played with the cousins up and down the valley. Losing her mama was sooo sad, but going to school and church and playing up and down the valley with so many cousins was lots of fun; and sometimes, she even forgot, for just a little while, how much she missed her

Betty Jean looked through the front windshield of the old truck. Through the fog she could see the outline of a log house. She could see someone standing on the porch! As they neared, she could see uncle sitting in his straight back chair with a pile of shavings on the porch nearby. He was whittling. Betty Jean thought surely that was a different pile of shavings than when they were here 2 years ago . . . . you never know . . . and it didn't matter

Dad pulled the red truck off the road into the side yard. Even the old red truck seemed to give one final groan of relief!

"Ohh, Sis!" Aunt was looking for them and she saw them coming. Aunt was at the truck as mama opened the door. Betty Jean thought her Aunt looked so tired. But, that didn't stop Aunt! She ran and threw her arms around Betty Jean's mother. There were times that Betty Jean wondered what it would be like to have a sister. The two women held on to each other for a few minutes, not saying a word. Were those tears going down mama's cheeks?

Aunt asked if they were more than tired. Had it been an awful long time on the road?

Her mother said, "No, it wasn't too bad at all.

Betty Jean thought to herself . . . Just ask me, I will tell you the truth.

As they began walking toward the cabin, Mother told Sister, "I've brought something for you."

Betty Jean could not imagine what it would be. There wasn't money to buy anything they didn't just HAVE to have . . . . And, Mother had brought a "present!"

Mother turned back to the old red truck. Dad was untying the package from the outside of the cab. He said "Just tell me where you want it."

"On the kitchen table" said mama. They all gathered inside the cabin. Mama untied the string from the outside of the package. Mama fretted. They HAD been on the road all day. She wrapped the string around a scrap of paper. Betty Jean knew mama would use that string another time. Betty Jean wondered what was in the package.

She heard her mother saying. "Sis, I know from your letters that your cows went dry and you haven't had fresh milk for ever so long. I hope this is still fresh. I tried to wrap it really good.

It was a jug! Mother had wrapped layers of newspaper around a milk jug before putting it into several brown grocery sacks. The jug held fresh milk. Mother knew the paper would keep it nice and cool on that long trip.

The jug still felt cool. Proudly, Mama unscrewed the lid and tipped the jug to pour the milk into the clean pitcher aunt had set on the table.

Betty Jean knew she would always remember the look of dismay on her mama's face when nothing came from the jug. Her mama looked inside the jug.

"Why it's butter!" she exclaimed. Those Arkansas washboard roads had churned the cold milk into fresh cool butter.

Both aunt and uncle vowed as how the one thing they could use more'n anything was fresh butter. Betty Jean was so happy they had decided to come. She had already forgotten how tired she felt when they arrived. Everyone should be as lucky as Betty Jean to get to ride in a cramped old red truck and ride over "wash board" roads to visit an "Arkansas aunt and uncle".

Soon they needed had to get back. The morning arrived. They were to leave the mountain. She wondered about her mama. So quiet until she came to Arkansas. Mama was different all right. Mama and her sister talked all day . . . and Betty Jean suspicioned all night! Yes, her mother was different. Coming to Arkansas had sure made a difference with mother.

Betty Jean got into the truck and waited on her mom and dad and brother. She felt she could do that just pretty good. Waiting that is; she could do that better than most. The others came and they were ready to begin the trip back to Oklahoma.

Betty jean looked back and saw uncle and aunt standing in the road. Somehow she knew Aunt would stay there until she could no longer see the truck.

That is when she noticed her mama. She wasn't talking. Betty Jean knew mama was different. Mama looked straight ahead, quietly staring into the distance.

Betty Jean looked at her mama and knew something was wrong. This was different. Betty Jean wasn't sure her mama was breathing. Betty Jean did not know what to think. Her dad wasn't saying anything, either. This was not the way to finish their wonderful trip! Betty Jean did the only thing she knew to do. She just scooted as far back on that old truck seat as she could scoot. She held her arms really close to her side and closed her eyes. Maybe when she opened her eyes she would know she had just had a dream. Somehow, she knew that wasn't going to happen. She closed her eyes as much as she could. She was 8 years old and she knew something was dreadful wrong.

Her dad saw her and said "Now, Bets, if you don't open your eyes you are going to miss all these things I'm a seeing. You done missed that deer back there . . . and see that fox going there! Look down that bluff. You can see a far piece through these mountains.

Betty Jean thought her dad could see more things. She didn't want to miss one of them. She was real busy for a while, looking from one side of the road to the other. Then . . . . she remembered mama.

She looked at her mama . . . and Betty jean was glad her mama was breathing now. Even if she didn't talk, at least she was mama again

All of a sudden, Betty Jean knew! She knew without being told. Arkansas was her Mother's home. Maybe that is why they didn't come real often. The coming was wonderful, it was the leaving that was almost more than Mother could manage to do. Going back home to that land that dared you to stay and carve out a living. Yet it would haunt you if you left!

They did return to Oklahoma. You know the years have a way of passing.

Betty Jean grew up and married and had a family.

Betty Jean's dad worked for a company, he retired after a few more years. He and Betty Jean's mama did not do an awful lot. They had worked so hard all their lives, they seemed content to just relax.

Betty Jean's mama and dad did take a few trips. You know where they went? They visited the kin folks in Arkansas.

It was not unusual for Betty Jean to get a post card from her mama. "Hi we're in Arkansas. See you soon"

One day, Betty Jean went to her mail box and there was a post card. It said "Hi, we are having a wonderful time; we'll be home by the time you get this card"

As she looked at the card, she thought about the last few times they had gone to see her mother and dad. They had seemed happy . . . happier than she could remember they being . . . even contented.

Betty Jean looked at the post card again. Why had SHE NOT NOTICED it before? We will be HOME it said. Her mama loved Arkansas. But she was coming HOME.

Betty Jean knew Arkansas would always hold a special place in mama's heart. But Mama had come to know Oklahoma as her home.

At the same time, Betty Jean as well as she knew her own name. Mama had come to realize how much she loved that long tall Cherokee she had married.

Ohh these folks were plain and simple folks. A lot like some of us here today. They came through this part of the country. I plan to tell you their names. You may have heard tell of these folks. More than likely you know someone who knew them . . . They were folks a lot like you and me.

Their names were Arthur and Frankie. Some called them Jum and Toots. But, well, they called me Betty Jean I want to thank you for reading about the summer I was 8 years old.

Beverly "Betty Jean" Brownn ca. 1950

Floy McCutcheon Home
Cave Creek, Arkansas

1952

Picture taken 1952 Joan Denton Martin sitting in foreground

Floy Casey McCutcheon Postmistress @
Cave Creek AR   Sister Faye Denton and
Frankie Brown

Post Office Sign above door entering add-on

Oliver and Floy McCutcheon home Cave Creek Arkansas

Uncle Oliver and Aunt Floy Casey McCutcheon lived in this house Aunt Floy was the post mistress at Cave Creek AR. Her Post Office was in the add-on to one side of main structure. Sign over the door indicates Post Office in this room. The add-on on opposite side was the kitchen.

Arthur and Frankie Brown lived in this house til Oologah Dam required relocation

Pencil drawing made by Howard Brown. Lived here at time of "Betty Jean Story" Mother had a box camera but rarely used it. I doubt there was money for film. Howard could do "anything" I thought. This looks so much like "home" When Oologah Dam was built; we were one family of many who had to relocate.

MARGARET HOUSTON
CASEY
BEAUTIFUL MAMA

Margaret's daughter, Frankie, was only 8 years old when Margaret died.

Frankie thought of her often. Frankie accepted but never quite understood why her wonderful mama had to leave her when she (Frankie) was so young. Margaret— Always Remembered Always Loved.

Margaret, who lived in Newton County, Arkansas her entire life 1874-1922, was my grandmother. I feel as though I knew her even though she died 23 years before I was born. Her parents were Harvey and Harriet (Blackwood) Houston.

Margaret Houston Casey

Margaret is buried at Buffalo Cemetery with her first grandchild, Floy's new born son, next to her.

SKETCH

NO! It Isn't
an Ice Cream Dish

I am going to tell you a story about someone. I knew her about as well as anyone knew her. She was very quiet. she did not say very much. I remember watching her read her bible.

It just seemed like mother could not adjust to life without dad. They had been married 42 ½ years when dad passed away.

Mother had never talked very much. Now, there were days of almost complete silence. She would respond or answer your question, but it was as though she did not know how to interact with you. Maybe it would get better, I thought. After all 42 ½ years was a long time. Especially when so many of those years were spent side by side with a "long tall Cherokee Indian" who was her "Strength of Gibralter".

Mother had come to visit. She had been at my house a week. We lived over an hour from her, and she knew it would be the next weekend before I could get away to take her home.

I knew she wanted to be home in her little house. What could I do to get her mind off her sadness? She had always loved to look for "hidden or secret treasures" at a rummage sale. When I grew up, few people had garages.so mother was not real familiar with a "garage sale" . . . but she sure knew what it was after she went to her first one! And she loved them!

Knowing there wld probably be a few garage sales near the week end, I told her we would go to one or two before I took her home. If she wanted to do that. She thought that was an outstanding idea.

She was ready to go to a garage sale. We took the newspaper and off we went. We stopped at the first one and were looking at the usual fare. There were children's clothing and a few dishes and glassware. She was standing next to the table with the glass ware when I heard the lady, who was operating the garage sale, tell another person, "I really don't know what that old glass piece is. I imagine it is a vase. It really looks old, doesn't it?" "But it somehow does not look like a vase, does it? I bet it is an ice cream dish" the second lady responded. I was surprised to hear mother say, "It isn't an ice cream dish"

Being a woman of few words, the sentence "hung in mid-air". At least that is how it appeared to me.

"Ohh, I don't know what else it would be" said the first lady. "If it isn't a vase . . . or an ice cream dish. It just has to be one or the other"

I noticed mother kept looking at the glass. She spoke again. "It is a napkin holder" I thought to myself. what is she talking about? Napkin holder?

One of the ladies said "Ohh, ma'am, I don't think so. I have never seen a napkin holder like this." She was kind, and mother didn't really appear to be offering any more information.Suddenly, mother said "Do you have any cloth napkins?"

I watched, knowing I was seeing something about mother I had noticed only rarely before. As though there was another "part" of her that she kept hidden.

But what about cloth napkins? I mean, we were lucky to have paper napkins.cloth napkins were never used at mother's house! I mean, she didn't even have running water. How would mother know about cloth napkins?

The lady told mother, "Sure, I have cloth napkins" She was being very kind.she looked at me as if to say. It is okay, we will just humor her. It isn't asking too much.

She returned with the cloth napkins and handed them to mother.

A few people were standing behind us. It began to get quiet . . . people were no longer talking to each other. They were simply watching in silence.

That is when it happened. Mother looked at the napkins laying on that table and she put her purse down. I watched as she took her work callused hands and gently picked up the napkins.

"You just lay the napkins down and stack them like this." She proceeded to do just that. "Then you pick them up and place them in the napkin holder. If you have stacked them properly, the napkins will come up one at a time when you gently tug on them by the corner." As she talked, she demonstrated how to place the napkins. Then, the test. She took a finger and thumb and very slightly tugged on the first corner, with a graceful turn of her wrist and hand, the napkin came up so very smoothly . . . then the second one.then the third one . . . then the fourth one.

Several people were watching. I was watching . . . but I was seeing not only a lady demonstrate a napkin holder. I knew I was watching my mother relive a memory of her child hood. A time when her dear mama taught her the basics of house keeping, of keeping a neat home. The basics mother had been forced to lay aside as she came to the rough and tough Indian Territory.

What else had she laid aside? Did I ask questions? I have been asked that more than once.

I asked no questions. I respected her privacy and felt privileged to have been there. Grateful that she "went back to her childhood" just for a few minutes in the garage of a person she did not know and would never see again.

I took mother home. She did not mention what had happened that morning. Always at peace, she seemed more so that day. Within a few months mother went to Glory.

"Yes, mother, you were right. It was not an ice cream dish nor was it a vase. It was your child hood memory and you got to live it just one more time before you went to Glory"

Thanks for the memories, Mother Dear, Thanks for the memories. Why am I telling you this story?

Mother grew up as the "apple of her daddy's eye" in a comfortable home. She came to Oklahoma, married, and had very little comfort thereafter.

Did she feel as though God left her? I don't think so. She had child hood memories; many she never shared with anyone.

She did share the important things; contentment. And NEVER BLAME OTHERS. She had the peace of living a Godly life.

You see—What she left was not as important as what she kept.

Was she blessed? I think she was. A husband who cared deeply for her. She has been gone for more than 35 years (as I write this sketch) this story about her life. It is in the hope that if one needs encouragement you will receive it.

Every day of her life, mother knew these words: Jeremiah 29:11 For I know the plans I have for you, plans for a future and a hope.

Yes, when she married, she left some things behind.but the most important she kept forever. I am so very thankful this lady was my mother!

Next page Mother's early School days. She and both older sisters attended this country school.taught by Mr.Walter Lackey, standing in the back row, taught at the college level, author of books incl. history of Newton Co AR.

1. Mother Frankie Casey m. Brown   Front row
2. Sis Faye m. Denton   Back row
3. Sis Floy m. McCutcheon   Back row
Teacher back row Mr. Walter Lackey

Newton CO Country School ca. 1920
Teacher is Walter Lackey - Author History of Newton County
Three daughters of Jesse & Margaret Casey are in the picture

Teacher became Professor Lackey well known author of his beloved
Newton County, Arkansas

About 1929 Picture taken on steps of Newton County Academy at Mount Parthenon, AR
Mother is in front row 3rd from left.   Frankie Casey Brown

My Mother, Frankie Casey, with class mates.
A Lady ... she was Margaret's daughter !

Frankie Casey Parthenon Arkansas

Mother

Mother above
about time she
graduated from
Newton Co Academy
Dad in CC
uniform

Arthur T Brown
Uniform worn in CC Camp

Dad

SKETCH

Anthony Casey and Louisa Richards Rutledge   Casey

Patriots—Their Honor is Earned

In late Sept 1880, Mr. Calvin Rutledge prepared for trip from Pleasant Hill, Boone Co AR, to Harrison to sell dried fruit. He asked his wife if she needed money but Elizabeth (nicknamed Louisa) Richards Rutledge was a frugal lady and told him "no". He asked if she wanted anything from town.

Elizabeth told him she needed a wash tub, a smoothing iron, a bolt of calico, and a bolt of brown domestic.

Calvin went into town. His wife and the younger children, including 3 month old Jeff, stayed home. Eldest son, Billy, went with his father. Calvin left Billy at his parent's home near Harrison. In Harrison, Calvin sold the wagon and team and asked his father to take him to Eureka Springs. This was the last any of his family ever saw Calvin Smith Rutledge.

A few years after this disappearance, he was seen at Enid, Oklahoma by a former Boone Co neighbor, Mr. Reed had gone to Indian Territory. At least, Mr. Reed thought it was Calvin Smith Rutledge that he saw . . . This man was known as Calvin Smith.

Mr. Reed walked over to the man and began talking with him. They had a nice chat. It was getting mid-day and Mr. Smith said he needed to go and tend to his horses, which were tethered at the edge of town. They would "visit" again shortly. Mr. Smith was never seen again.

And therefore sums up the life {as we know it} of Calvin Smith Rutledge. Who knows if there was a family before Louise Richards?

Elizabeth {Louise} Rutledge was left with 7 children ages 3 mos. to 17 yrs. She share cropped in vicinity of Mt Judea, Newton Co AR. She weighed less than 100 pounds but reared her family through persistent determination.

She raised those children and later in life married Mr. Anthony Casey, a well to do farmer. This kind man made her last years easy and comfortable.

Louisa's daughter, Clara Jerusha Davis, wrote that "Uncle Anthony" was so good to her mother. She writes "we were all happy to see her take life easy since she had had such a difficult time while she was bringing up her family. She was a devout Christian. She lived her religion every day."

Elizabeth {Louisa} died of blood poisoning in 1906.

More about Anthony Casey: Born in Tennessee in 1826, he was in Arkansas by 1836. He came by wagon train to settle a country which did not want to be settled. He served for the Union Troops. He was admitted to a Little Rock AR hospital for pneumonia. He was released after one month. Later, he was in the Small Pox Hospital for three weeks. Again this was at Little Rock. He served Company E, 2nd Arkansas Infantry, from 1863 to 1865.

He heard of his friends and kin being tortured and killed by bushwhackers as he was doing what he felt he should do for his country. He returned to his beloved Newton Co AR to learn of longtime friends leaving wives as widows and children as orphans.

Did this enter his mind as he married at 71 years of age? Undoubtedly. We can only learn of these things and shudder at the sacrifices our ancestors have made for us. God is sooo good to allow me to learn of this story more than 100 years after it happened!

Anthony Casey was my great great grandfather.

John William Rutledge, one of the abandoned children, was my great uncle as he married my grandmother's sister.

Also, Anthony Casey did something he might be surprised if he could somehow know this one little kindness for a black man would be remembered 100+ years later.

When Anthony Casey came to Arkansas he was accompanied by a black "slave". Anthony was only about 10 years old when his family came to Arkansas by wagon train . . . so this black boy and Anthony probably grew up "together". This must have been one of those "special" friend situations.

When the black man (no idea of his name) died where would he be buried? At this time, black people were buried in their cemeteries just as they had their own schools. No such cemetery anywhere around in Newton Co Arkansas. So, Anthony took his friend and went to the edge of the Buffalo Cemetery. [1] There he dug a grave for the man. He did not stop after the burial. Anthony knew sentiments were deep in the community. So, just to be sure his long time friend would rest in peace, Anthony placed rocks on the grave . . . . not just a few, but many. An honorable resting place for an honorable friend . . . . no matter what others thought. [2]

We must not forget . . . BUT FIRST WE MUST LEARN of the blessings that ours because they chose to die for us knowing they would never see us . . . this side of "glory"

---

[1] Buffalo Cemetery is near Parthenon, Arkansas . . . Newton County. Steps are in front of Buffalo Church next to cemetery. Many Casey family members are here. The oldest stone is dated 1840. Mary Casey was Bev's grandmother several generations back.

[2] Pauline Brown daughter of Lattie Casey >William Uriah Casey>Anthony Casey

Main Source from Ozark Cousins by Bud Phillips.

Addtns per Beverly Brown Hart Copy of letter written by Clara Jerusha Davis was given to me by Cecilia Houston Campbell. Clara Jerusha Rutledge married John Newton Davis; who was the son of Benton Columbus Davis and Mary Blackwood Davis. Mary Blackwood Davis was sister of Harriett Blackwood Houston. Harriett Houston was my great grandmother.

Picture taken from steps of Buffalo Church near Mount Parthenon, AR. Cemetery is on the right.

Cemetery on the right.

Picture taken from front steps of Buffalo Church near Mount Parthenon, AR

Front Door of Buffalo Church.
Cemetery next door has tombstone (the oldest stone in cemetery) of Mary Casey.
Bev is descendant of Mary Casey.

I love this picture

Every time I see these steps; middle of these steps worn from footsteps going inside to Worship. Most lovely sight to see

SKETCH

There is a Panther
On the Mountain

S amuel Hudson was born about 1811 in the grand old state of Tennessee. His parents came to Lawrence Co AR before traveling on to Newton Co AR

About 1832, Samuel Hudson settled above Jasper AR. Some folks say he was the first white settler.

Samuel cut his way through the unbroken forest, which was inhabited by Indians and wild animals.

He finally located on the creek three miles above Jasper and became very successful; wealthy by some standards.

He prospered and followed farming and stock raising exclusively until 1860 when he built a gristmill above Mount Parthenon. He operated this until 1873 when he built a mill on site, which later was site of Matlock's mill. Operated this mill for 8 yrs. until his death in 1881.

Samuel was commissioner of public buildings of Newton Co prior to the war.

He was a Royal Arch Mason and a Democrat.

Samuel affiliated with the Methodist Episcopal Church South.

Samuel was an expert marksman and delighted in hunting. One day he killed four bears and five deer. This day stood out in his repertoire of tales. That is until the day he went to cut down the "bee tree".

This day was so eventful that Samuel Hudson would never forget it. It began innocently enough. This was the day Samuel and his son had a "mission". They were going to cut down a "bee tree". Why Sam and his son could taste the honey on hot biscuits already! And the honey comb. That was what the little brothers and sisters were always wanting. Today maybe they could get lots of comb as well as the honey.

But, this day Samuel would "meet" a panther. Samuel and eldest son, a young lad, went into the woods about two miles from the house to cut down a bee tree. Samuel had just begun working when looking up the ravine, he saw an immense panther gliding along. Waiting until the animal was within a few yards of him, he threw a rock at it. Samuel thought the rock would kill the panther.

The rock missed; another one was thrown. Each time the rock came at the panther, the animal would jump and snap at the stones. The panther had not seen Samuel Hudson YET!

Samuel grasped his axe and made a slight noise to get the panther's attention. Success . . . .

The panther stood still, then slowly approached Samuel. The panther moved his long tail from side to side, crouched for a moment, and leaped through the air to land on Samuel Hudson. The panther had Samuel's head in its jaws. Samuel desperately dealt the panther a blow with his axe. The axe slipped from his hands and was on the ground.

Samuel managed to free his head from the jaws of the panther and a terrific struggle between man and beast occurred on the side of that beautiful Ozark mountain. Samuel had a knife in his pocket but could not reach it. Then Samuel remembered. For the first time, Samuel had brought a butcher knife with him. He had planned to use the butcher knife when he was "working the bee tree". Desperately Samuel ordered his young son to get him the butcher knife.

The boy handed Samuel the butcher knife; Samuel took the knife, knowing that not only his life, but the life of his son depended on him! Where would he get the strength to plunge the knife into the panther. Samuel could feel, as well as see, the blood dripping from his body on to the ground.

Samuel, with a strength that comes only times of extreme agony, plunged the butcher knife into the panther time after time. The animal finally loosed his hold and fell dead at his feet.

Samuel, deeply lacerated, knew he would bleed to death if he did not receive help soon. Samuel assured his young son that he could what had to be done. Keeping his wits, Samuel told son what to do.

Samuel's son managed to bandage the wounds enough to slow the bleeding. As gently as possible, he carried his father back to the cabin. Samuel did recover from his "Meeting with the Panther"!

Additional: Samuel Hudson's first wife was the mother of 13 children. This dear lady died and left Samuel alone. Samuel told his friends and family he was going to go hunt for a "ginner" to help him in the mill.

When Samuel returned, he brought his "ginner". "She" was Sarah Blackwood. Sarah Blackwood was the widow of James Blackwood who was killed by bushwhackers as he worked in the field in Newton Co AR. Sarah Carolina Wheeler Blackwood had lost her husband and her husband's brother to the Bushwhackers during the Great UnCivil War. Her father in law, James Blackwood, was tortured by having his feet held in the coals of the fireplace. Sarah Wheeler Blackwood had three small children when she married Samuel Hudson.

Samuel had sired 13 children {at least 13 as the infant mortality rate was so high then} before he married Sarah Blackwood. Then there were 3 more children, at least.

Sarah's son, James Blackwood, had every right to believe his step father would not notice him. Why should he?

James knew Samuel Hudson had rescued his mother from a much "harder" life by marrying her. James was appreciative . . . that was enough.

Little did James comprehend that Samuel Hudson was indeed a man above most men. Sam did notice young James Blackwood. More than that. He recognized within the young man whose father had been murdered; there beat a spirit of his Indian ancestors! A spirit that wanted to go to medical school and return to minister and treat his kinfolk in Newton Co.

Samuel Hudson helped James Blackwood's dream come true. Samuel Hudson did, indeed, send James Blackwood to medical school. James spent the remainder of his life among his kin and friends as he was known as their "family doctor".

Up to this point my story has been true as far as can tell. I have read the accounts of these happenings.

This next part of the saga I happen to know is true because I was part of it. A few years ago, we took a car trip to Newton County,

Arkansas. My cousin and her husband and my husband and I were in search of the final resting place of my great, great grandfather James Blackwood. I had been told he was buried in what the locals called "The Old Indian Graveyard".

We were on the right mountain . . . but we needed to be on the other side! Looking at a road map I could see a road which went from where we were up and around the mountain. By taking this road we should reach our destination much sooner than if we turned and went back to the main highway.

We were at the crossroads of two gravel roads on a lazy Saturday afternoon. We had left the paved road some miles back. There was a tiny store with 3 teenagers standing in front. There was a lone gas pump standing in front of the tiny building. Couple of other buildings. Probably once a place of business . . . it had become . . . like untold numbers of tiny communities a memory more than anything else.

Not wanting to get on to a road which we could not "navigate" with our car, we looked at the map intently. The line indicating the road was straight . . . not broken line. Uhhh, knowing we needed to be cautious. Last thing we needed was to have trouble on the road with the car! We better ask someone just to be sure before we traveled farther down a seldom traveled road.

We had turned down the road in question, but stopped. Husband turned around the car around and went back a couple of blocks to the store where the teens were gathered. We asked "If we take that road across that road, will we get to Cowell?"

"Sure" one teen replied.

"Sure, just stay on that road, you can't miss it!" his friend joined in.

Did I detect a sparkle in their eyes? My imagination, I am sure.

Once again, we turned down the road. I looked back and saw the teens were still standing in front of the little store. They seemed to be watching us as we drove away.

The road was gravel, within 1 block we could see the gravel was disappearing from the middle of the road. Also, the road was narrowing unbelievable soon. Within ¼ of a mile it was apparent if we met another vehicle there was no room to turn around.

Decision to be made. We could back up or continue. Ahead we went. This might be only a temporary part of the road. After all, the road looked so good on the map. AND, the boys had assured us we went going the right direction.

Cousins Joan and Floyd Martin were with Max and I as we traveled, at no more than 15 m p h. Why were we traveling so slowly? Would we call this a logging road? We were in a National Forest, so no commercial logging road here! What were we traveling? We looked up at the sky to find only an occasional shaft of light. The massive timber formed an umbrella above us and around us.

The road which began as narrow gravel road and narrowed to a single country lane was dirt and boulders. It had become a tiny track which had been worn over decades. This was probably a fire lane . . . The road had been traveled by wagon or trucks, nature had helped no doubt by washing the dirt away from all except the largest boulders.

The car was almost idling as we continued. No way we could back down the road! The afternoon was passing. Looking out the windows of the car, I saw not the trunks of the pines and oaks, but the massive ROOTS of the timber which loomed over us. Anxiously I peered into the front to glance at the gas gauge! If we had a flat tire . . . how would we even be able to get out of the car much less change a tire? Before the days of common cell phones, the only persons who knew we were on this road were the boys. Now I knew the sparkle in the boy's eye was not my imagination. It was Saturday afternoon fun for some country teens with time on their hands!

I felt we were okay; but I began praying we would get to the end of the road before the blackness of night enveloped us. It was already getting even darker . . . and we were only late afternoon. In a couple of hours, it would be dark in the midst of the forest. A forest which was unknown to us.

That is when it happened! I do not know that I have ever been more in awe as a large black panther ran down the hill and lunged across the road in front of us. He moved with deliberation but slow and with grace.

As though the cat were making sure we knew we were "intruders". He leaped from one side of the boulder strewn trail to the other with seemingly no effort. The cat could have touched the car, but he chose to merely turn his head and look at us through the windshield. I saw his eyes. His ancestors and ours had been enemies. He had remained. Again, was I imagining? I think not. We were the intruders. We must not stay. We could look, but we must remove ourselves from the mountain. We must go. It is the way it has to be. We must go. Make no mistake. We must go.

This was the panther's home. Stories have been told about panthers. Local folk told of the panthers that used to inhabit the forest. Some would vow the cats still roamed at night when no one could see them. Many doubted that. Surely the hunters had done away with those big cats. I have heard that even the locals have tried in vain to sight the mighty black cat!

I can personally attest that this panther was indeed real. We (Oklahoma People) truly did acknowledge we were visitors who were allowed just a glimpse of the beauty of a wild animal . . . whose ancestors shared the mountain with our ancestors!

As the gas gauge was getting very low and the darkness was unbelievable according to our watches, we could see light up ahead. We saw a power pole! There was civilization close by, surely!

As we came to the end of that narrow road there was a house that appeared to have been there for many many years. The dear Mr. and Mrs. were standing on the porch. They appeared to be looking in the direction we had come. Had the boys decided their trick might have disastrous results? We don't know.

The Mr. And Mrs. were so nice. We had arrived just where we had hoped. We told them why we had traveled to Arkansas. They didn't know much about Indian Cemeteries. The Mister "allowed" as there was cemeteries all over that country.

"What name ya say ya looking fer?" he said.

Joan and I told him our families' names from Newton County included Houston, Casey, and Blackwood. We had been told our great great grandfather, James Blackwood, was buried at Cowel. We knew he was not at the cemetery on the highway. There must be another one.

He looked at us and said "Bout dark. Light gonna fade perty quick. Don't know if it be any help to ye. But they be few graves out back of the barn. I keep it fenced to keep the cows away from the stones. Don't seem right to have livestock trampling the graves. If you'ns watch your step, I'll show you where they lay. You be sure and look where you walking. City folks ferget and get plumb made when they step in them cow patties."

We looked at each other. We had come this far; traveled over a logging trail; we figured we could walk through cow patties.

He walked in front and we followed. The farmer told the truth. Mighty careful we were. Fence had no gate. The fellows held the barbed wire as we crawled between the strands. We stood straight and looked across the tombstones. Directly in front of us was the stone we were trying to find. James Blackwood had passed over 100 years earlier. We stood on top of the mountain near his final resting place. The black panther's descendants still lived here. James Blackwood had been found. But we found more. Ohh, yes!

We found what we had hoped to find and so much more. Simply hoping to find something of our human roots . . . so to speak, we were allowed to touch and glimpse a part of our heritage which few are allowed to do.

Only God can allow such glimpses.

I am so thankful we were allowed ours.

sources: *main source Goodspeed Reminiscent History Ozark Region, Bud Phillips Ozark Cousins, with additional by Beverly Brown Hart. Bev's grandmother was first cousin to DR James Blackwood.*

SKETCH

A Woman Plain and Simple
She Kept a Secret
for 40 years

I will tell you, as I begin, this is a true story. I know because I became a part of it. Didn't even realize it; that is how it had to be. Because if I knew, I would probably ask questions that she could not answer, not then; hopefully never.

First, let me tell you about the day I first knew about the secret. We were visiting at my parent's home. Beautiful blue sky; it was absolutely gorgeous. After all these years, I can still remember the sound of the gravel crunching underneath the tires as we pulled into my parent's drive.

Husband and I sat on the couch, as usual. I knew dad wasn't feeling well these days, but I just could not admit it might be anything not to be expected.

Suddenly, Dad looked at my mother and said, "Toots, I think you had better show Betty the picture"

Mother never moved from her chair. Ever silent, she looked straight ahead and then down at the floor. Not too unusual for mother. No emotion showed on her face. There was nothing to indicate what was going through her mind. I know now, that this was the day she had dreaded . . . after 40 years; the day had arrived.

Again Dad said quietly, but firmly "Toots, I think you had better show Betty the picture."

By this time I was thoroughly confused. "What PICTURE!" I wanted to say; but said nothing.

He didn't say it aloud where I could hear; but mother knew. I did not.

He was actually saying "Toots, You have got to trust somebody. You MUST show Betty the picture. She is your daughter. You can trust her." Mother could hear him as if he spoke audibly. I could hear not a word.

Mother got up from her chair, walked slowly to the dining room where she removed a picture from the wall behind the wood heating stove.

This is not making sense. I have seen that picture all my life. It was about 20 inches long X 14 inches high. Just a picture from an old magazine. In the picture were Abraham Lincoln, wife Mary Todd Lincoln and their sons. I did not remember a time the picture was not hanging on the wall.

Mother laid the picture face down on her lap. Still, she had not spoken a word. She had picked up a pair of wire pliers from somewhere. She took the pliers and began removing the small tacks./ Very deliberate; almost as though in slow motion. What was she thinking? What was going on here, I thought to myself.

After she had removed the tacks, she removed the brown paper which covered the back of the picture; the cardboard spacers. She removed the picture of Abraham Lincoln's family. Next, it appeared she was replacing all of it! This made less sense every minute. Dad said not a word.

Was she placing that stiff cardboard behind the glass?

Mother raised the picture to face me. But, first she glanced at the picture before turning it to face me.

I had never seen this picture. It was a man in a very old picture. He appeared to be sitting for the picture.

I asked quietly, "Who is this?"

Mother said, "This is a charcoal painting of my grandfather, Harvey Houston. He was mama's papa." She held that picture ever so briefly; then began putting the picture back together and placed it in the frame.

Mother placed the picture on the dining room wall in exactly the same spot it had been. It was a picture of Abraham Lincoln's family; not the picture I had just seen.

Mother came back into the living room.

No one said a word. Finally, she said "Mama told me this story. Her papa {mother's Grandpa} would not agree To have his picture painted. One day, Grandma Harriett told her husband, Harvey, the traveling painter would be coming by their house. They both knew he was on the mountain. Grandma knew he was in the neighborhood. If Harvey would hold that horse he was so proud of . . . why they would get a picture of that magnificent animal.

Now Harvey was proud of his horses. He had a reputation of having some of the finest horses in the state. Harvey stood close to the horse to keep him from being startled as the painter began using his charcoal to draw the picture.

The children were going about their chores, occasionally whispering to one another. Harvey did not notice.

As the time passed, Harriett began to doubt her plan. What if it turned out badly. The children knew what she had done. She had tricked their father. Ohh My! No, she was not at all sure she had done the right thing.

It was just before dinner time. {In those days the noon meal was dinner, the evening meal being supper} The portrait painter stood back to view his work. He nodded his head as though he was pleased. Finished at last! Next was the true test. He could not remember ever doing a picture in this manner before. He called for Harriett to come out so Harvey and she could look at the portrait.

Only then did Harvey learn he was the subject of the Day's painting.

Harvey felt his face grow red. He had been tricked, duped! His wife had outwitted him! Did his sons and daughters know? Were they aware of the deception their mother had devised? Harvey knew the joke would be well known all over the mountain. He looked at Harriett. That Indian woman!

Suddenly Harvey chuckled as he thought of how he had held that horse so very still for the portrait. The joke was certainly on him. And Harriett, the Indian woman he had married!

Harvey thought all she wanted was a picture of him Even since the camera had been in use, she would not look at the camera. Her people were suspicious of the box which gave off sound and smoke when taking a picture. Harriett would turn her head and not look directly at the camera. And, she did this to him. This trickery!

As quickly as his flushed face reflected his anger, the Scotsman smiled at Harriett. The joke was on him. But, the best thought was not a new one. He knew he was one lucky man to have this Cherokee as his wife. The story would be all over the mountain, and he would be the one telling it!

What more did mother say about the picture? She said Not another word about it. She busied herself with household chores as though nothing had happened. She went outside into the yard.

I looked at dad. From the look of his eyes, I knew that I had learned all I would learn this day. There was not so much secrecy as a hint of sadness and deep thought. He was thinking about mother. I would not intrude.

I left that day with unspoken, unanswered questions, perhaps some day there would be answers, perhaps not.

What happened to the picture? Well, Dad went to Glory in 1974. The next year, Mother joined him. After their passing, I told my two brothers I would like to have the picture of Harvey Houston.

They both responded, "Sure, but what are you talking about?" Neither knew mother's secret. Somehow I was not surprised.

Now it was my turn. I went to the wall and removed the picture from the wall. I did just as mother had done a couple of years earlier. This time it was different. This time when the picture was put into the frame, behind the glass, Harvey was in front. It was time . . . . you see he had waited for over 40 years.

Of course, I have been asked why she did that. For several years the story had to stop there. I had copies made, gave copies to whatever family member wanted one, at no charge. But I honestly could not tell them why it had been where it had been nor when mother acquired it.

When the time was right, I would know more. If that time did not come, that was okay.

I also knew IF Dad had not insisted that Saturday afternoon, the picture would have never been shown. I don't think she could have forced herself to do it . . . were it not for that long tall Cherokee she had married.

Many years passed, perhaps 15 or 20. My husband and I and my cousin and her husband were going to AR. There was a family reunion.

The people were mother's cousins. Cousin and I had been invited but had never attended.

I had several pictures, some from mother's album. Some from her dad's album. I hoped someone would be able to identify them. I had resigned myself to not ever knowing any more about the "mysterious Harvey".

We arrived. Visited with a few people. I found myself at a table with mother's cousin. I had hoped to see her. I had never met her. Mother had spoken of her. I asked Ambolene if she knew who the pretty girl in the picture could be.

Ambolene, so stooped and the white hair which revealed her years, looked at the picture of the beautiful young girl.

"Sure, that's me" she said. "See that dress? That is my graduation dress. Your mama made it for me. She could make anything on a sewing machine. Her hair, your mama always had the prettiest hair. We were best friends as well as cousins. Did you know that?"

She hesitated and in the straightforward manner of a mountain woman, she looked closely at me . . . right into my eyes.

I held her gaze without wavering, but said not a word. Was she deciding what to say to me?

She said, "You know, even when I heard this I just did not believe it. I have always wanted to ask someone who could tell me. Did Frankie really take those things?"

I looked at her. "What did you say?"

"Did she really take those quilts from her papa's house? That just wasn't Frankie. But what else could have happened to them? They were made by her mama . . . but I never could believe my cousin and best friend would do that."

I assured her that I had never seen a quilt made by my grandmother. As far as I knew that had not happened. She seemed satisfied.

The day was almost over. We were in our car traveling back toward Harrison where we had motel rooms.

Something "felt wrong" . . . . as though I was missing something.

I kept thinking about the conversation with cousin Ambolene as cousin and visited, suddenly I knew . . . I looked at cousin.

I told her. "Did you hear what she said? She told us why Harvey was hidden for 40 years! I can't believe it, after all these years."

Cousin said, "What are you talking about? Ambolene couldn't even remember most of the people you mentioned. You didn't say anything about the mysterious charcoal portrait of our great great grandfather."

"Ohh, she told us all right. She nor you nor I knew what we heard. Remember, I had not learned until the year before mother died that mother had a stepmother." Cousin knew. Her mother {mother's sister had told her daughters}.

There was tension and strife between my mother and her stepmother. I will say no more about that. I honestly can only guess because mother simply would not discuss it. Just the way it was. Mother would have every reason to believe her papa would not be inclined to listen to what his youngest daughter had to say; my mother feared her mama's things would be destroyed; papa would be sorry; it would be too late.

As I had visited with Ambolene that afternoon I had forgotten about the coarse coverlet which now belonged to me. A coverlet which mother's papa and mama had planted the cotton, picked the cotton. Her mama had spun the thread, wove that thread on a narrow loom to make a bed coverlet. It was NOT a quilt. I had not made the connection.

I remembered Mother saying "See the seam? That is because mama's loom was narrow."

My cousins had given that coverlet to mother after their mama (who was mother's sister) died. They did not want it. Mother took it and said she thought "Betty might like to have it."

When she handed it to me, she said "There were two others, guess they disappeared."

It was coming together. Mother knew there were 3 to begin with because that is how many she removed from her papa's house . . . that last time she was there.

Probably she was thinking as she walked down that gravel road to her papa's house. She was leaving this valley she loved so dearly. There was other choice. The valley was too small for her and the woman her papa had married. Sooo different from her gentle mama . . . how could he do it.

No one was home, she had though the house would be empty. Papa lost most of his holdings in the "crash". He had just enough remaining to build this substantial home for "her". Enough daydreaming, she had to hurry.

Frankie swung open the wooden gate in the middle of the board picket fence. She walked up the lovely front path and turned before she put her foot on the first step. She turned to look out over the view. Her papa had chosen a beautiful spot to build this house. As far as the eye could see was a valley with hints of smoke spirals from home located up and down the valley and on the side of the far mountain. Would she see it again?

She turned back and walked up the front steps and stepped onto the deep porch which spanned the entire front of the home. She walked into the house and to the back room where they were kept. She picked up 3 coverlets from the shelf. She would not tarry, she turned to leave the house. She knew what she was doing. She walked through the living room, straight toward the front door. She did not come to pry or to meddle. She came to do what she had to do.

It caught her eye. The picture; everyone knew the story. Frankie's beautiful mama had been there that day. The day Grandma Harriett had "played a trick" on Grandpa Harvey. Her mama LOVED that picture. It had been in her Grandpa Harvey's house for 20 years, her mama and papa's house for 30 years.

Hesitating briefly, she took the picture down from the wall and walked out the front door. She would never return. She never stepped foot in that house again.

Frankie went to her sister's house just down the road. Sister could not believe what her younger sister had done. "It isn't worth it, honey. It isn't worth it."

NO, she would not return any of this. Sister wanted no part of it. Frankie saw a magazine. She knew what she would do. She opened the magazine and saw it. It was a picture of Abraham Lincoln's family. Her papa loved Abraham Lincoln and everything about the man. Now, we know what she did with that picture. She put both the magazine picture and the charcoal portrait in the one frame. It would be 40 years before she saw her grandfather's portrait again. The next time she saw it was when she showed it to me.

Mother brought the coverlets to Oklahoma when she came. Oldest sister wanted nothing to do with them. Frankie would see if middle sister wanted one of the coverlets. Middle sister did not either; but middle sister was always and forever a "Peace Maker". Middle sister agreed to put the coverlets in a trunk. She would never use them

Mother kept the picture. It had to be evident she took it only to protect it . . . that meant she would not look at it. Frankie knew if she looked at the portrait there would be questions. Her children; how would she tell her children that she took something to protect it, not destroy it. For 40 years she dreaded telling them; how could she take a chance her children would not understand. After all those years, Frankie could remember oldest sister telling her, "Honey, it isn't worth it!"

You see Frankie (my mother) had lived her life to protect her mama's beloved possession. But, Frankie wasn't thinking about her mama's integrity and honesty. That was even more precious than the charcoal portrait.

So the outcome is in the perspective of the one who hears or reads this story.

From my perspective, my mother walked the walk and was true to her talk. Rest my beloved mother, rest in peace.

As Dad told you, "You have to show her, Toots, You have to tell someone. Time is running out. She is your daughter. You can trust her."

That is why the charcoal portrait was hidden for 40 years. Mother could protect it. She could not look at it or enjoy owning it.

Following pictures include

Magazine (2 page picture) Abraham Lincoln family. This is what was in front of Houston portrait. I had this professionally framed. The framer managed to tear it down the middle! I am sure paper was so old it was difficult to handle.

Harvey Houston Charcoal portrait

W C Houston. Mother said "Uncle Billy worked in the timber cutting logs. One day he was walking by the side of a large timber truck or trailer which had huge logs tied on with chain. The chain broke and Uncle Billy was killed instantly. Uncle Billy had not married". Group picture. No information re: group.

Harvey and Harriett Houston
Jesse and Margaret Casey
letter telling Margaret her papa had died.

I had been to Cowel, Ark and saw the marker with Harvey Houston's name. One day I mentioned to Mother about her grandfather, Harvey Houston, being buried at Cowel. She told me "Harvey went to Indian Territory to stay with his son, Floyd Houston. Harvey was living with Floyd Houston when he died." I never dreamed the man had TWO tombstones.

HARVEY HOUSTON
Charcoal Portrait Which was in my mother's home
for 40+ years . . . hidden

Harvey and Harriett (Blackwood) Houston

Harriett is not looking into the camera . . . .
Harvey has "no problem" with it!

Mother's beloved papa and mama
Jesse Columbus Casey
Margaret Ann Houston Casey

W C Houston {Son of Harvey and Harriet Blackwood Houston} Chancel, AR

Written on back in pencil
W C Houston chancel, Arkansas

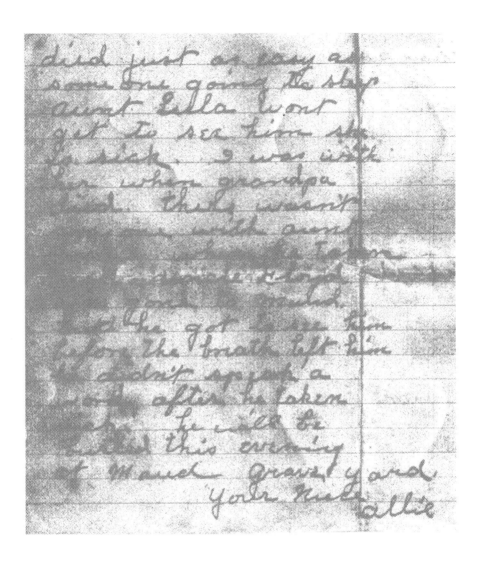

Letter sent to grandmother (Margaret Houston Casey) when her papa died. Harvey Houston died and is "being buried this evening at Maud graveyard." Harvey has markers at Maud Ok and Cowel, AR Letter in mother's photo album

SKETCH

These Things I Remember About Mama

Frankie Casey Brown . . . I remember she had a favorite "saying". For instance, she would say "If wishes were horses, we would all ride" I really didn't completely understand, and one day asked my dad what that meant. He said that when he and mother were "growing up" people didn't always have a horse to ride. Lots of people would ride a mule or ride in a wagon behind a team. To have a riding horse was to have something "extra". So . . . Everybody had wishes . . . . and if Everybody had as many horses as they had wishes they would have something!

And . . . I remember a plaque she had on the wall in the dining room. It said "Even a fish wouldn't get caught if he kept his mouth shut". (I now know that was a saying of Mark Twain's)

When I was in "a wanting mood"; mother "reminded" me of the little girl who cried because she had no shoes, until she saw the little girl who had no feet . . . .

I remember mother would "save" the battery in the radio. The battery was so different from batteries of today. The size for one thing! It was almost as big as a small shoe box and heavy!

She wouldn't turn on the radio unless she "really" wanted to hear it. She would listen every week day afternoon to a music show. I think the radio program came from Coffeyville, Ks. She would listen and how she enjoyed when they sang "It is No Secret what God Can Do" . . . . what He has done for others, He'll do for You . . . I can see mother now, standing over the cook stove, and listening to the radio.

One of Mother's favorite songs was by Porter Wagoner. It was entitled "Satisfied Mind" She also loved to hear Patti Page sing "Mockingbird Hill".

We lived not far from the Verdigris River on what was known as the Van Winkle Place. No electricity! {see pencil drawing of the house— Betty Jean Story}

I remember seeing mother buy oil cloth from a store in Nowata, OK to put on the dining table.

I remember seeing mother buy grey men's socks by the box in Nowata. I do not remember if the box held one dozen or half a dozen. I think it was Leader's Dept. store. The socks were for my dad and they were a brand called "Bachelor's Friend"

I remember mother taking the eggs to town to sell, even though she could have used them in cooking.

I remember going with mother to pick blackberries. We would walk to the berry patch early in the morning and pick until mid-morning. Yes, there were chiggers, and poison ivy. and an occasional snake. But, after going home, she would can those berries and make a cobbler for supper. She was just beginning HER day of "working the berries"! I "hated" those berry picking trips! Haven't gone again since I grew up! Soooo hot and not even a fan; never heard of one really.

I remember going with mother to pick up pecans in the fall. It was cooler and I didn't mind that as bad! Yes, we sold most of those, too.

I remember when the drought came, and the well ran low on water. We would gather all containers we had and load them in the pickup. When we went to town on Saturday, we would fill the containers with water at the hydrant at the feed store.

There was a zinc tub kept under the eaves of the house, the rain water we used to wash our hair. If the water wasn't used pretty soon, dad would begin to "holler" saying it was breeding mosquitoes!

I remember mother at the sewing machine. It was a treadle machine. We did not get electricity (in the river bottom) until I was about 10 yrs. old. She would wind the bobbin thread on an oblong bobbin and she could sew beautifully on that treadle machine. I did not have a "store bought" dress until I was 16 yrs. old. I had "store bought" underclothes, but mother made hers.

I remember each spring how thankful mother would be when the sun would feel so warm on our backs and our face when we were outside.

I remember helping mother put the wash kettle over the wood and sticks; lighting the fire and waiting for the water to be hot so we could wash the clothes. She washed the white clothes first, then the colored ones. My job was to use a broom handle and poke the clothes down under the water when they would float to the top. When the wind was blowing I always tried to be where the smoke would not get in my eyes. I still remember how my eyes would sting from the smoke! She used bluing which came in a little cardboard box. They looked like small blue marbles.

It was so hard to wash in the winter. She would try and wait for a warm day . . . The clothes would freeze before they would dry. I remember coming in from school and see laundry, behind the wood stove, where she was trying to dry it.

These are the things which remind me of how hard she worked, the long hours she labored.

I remember her rare smile. How she placed apples in a bushel basket and left them at the end of the drive . . . or road . . . for the preacher to pick up when he went by. He knew they were for him. No one else ever picked them up.

I can never forget the hours she had worked before the sun ever rose; the steps she walked as she never drove a car. I will never forget the quiet wisdom of a lady who wore dignity as naturally as she breathed.

Mother never lost all of her "Arkansas accent". She used perfect grammar; never using the "Arkansas hillbilly jargon". But once in a while she pronounced words differently. For example, one day I was asking about her family. Mother certainly was not going to volunteer any information I knew her mama was beautiful. I asked mother to tell me about Margaret Houston Casey. Mother was so young when Margaret died, she could not remember a lot. Mother finally said, "Mama was from across the hurriken" I asked again. Mother had little patience with me. Or so I thought . . . . often. She repeated the word slowly as though sounding out the word for a 5 year old child. I gave up. Margaret was from Newton County, Arkansas. That would have to do.

On one of our autumn vacations, we were driving through Newton Co, AR. Mother had passed on, but Newton Co remains one of my favorite places. Max was driving and we both enjoyed the trees and autumn colors. As we traveled across a bridge I began to say loudly. "That's it! That's it"

"What's it?"

"Hurriken. Mother said her mama was from across the hurriken. I never understood. Now I know. The sign at the end of the bridge. It spelled Hurricane River. Mother was saying hurriken, no hint of the "a" vowel. Mystery solved. But there would be more mysteries. That is fine, mother. I am blessed to have you for my mother. I still talk to you. Sometimes I listen better than when you were here.

When I was about 12 years old, I remember asking mother, "Columbus is sure a strange name. Wonder if my grandpa like his name?"

She immediately replied, "Why yes, papa did like his name. You see, when I was a little girl I wondered the very same thing and I asked him, "Papa, do you like your middle name, Columbus?"

Her papa said, "Well. Frankie, I guess I do like my middle name. If I didn't like it, I would change it." Somehow I knew he would have done exactly that!

Mother loved to visit her sisters, Floy Casey McCutcheon and Faye Casey Denton.

Aunt Floy lived at Cave Creek, Arkansas. She operated the post office from a room attached to her log house. I just thought that was the "coolest" thing! That post office and the wall paper in her kitchen. The wall was papered with newspapers. At the time Aunt Floy and Uncle Oliver lived at Cave Creek it was a "hard to make a living" country.

Aunt Floy knew she needed mail to go through that office to justify it remaining open. I grew up knowing mother would get at letter from her sister every day. If things were slow at the post office mother would get two letters. After I married I received a letter from Aunt Floy each day. My "newly married husband" thought that was something to get a letter from the same person every day. Sometimes the letter began Dear Betty, not much new here. Bye Aunt Floy. Once in a while it began Dear Peggy or Dear Joan. She was writing to her other nieces. Sometimes the letters got in the wrong envelopes!

Aunt Faye was married to Bill Denton. My first memory of them was when they lived at Old Alluwe. The first time I saw a television set was at their house. I even remember the first tv commercial. It was for table salt. It would even pour in the rain. Their house had a staircase. Cousins, Joan and Peggy, would play with me on the stairs. Both those girls were so nice to me. I loved them both.

Uncle Bill Denton had a motor boat. I thought that was neat. Mother said Aunt Faye was one of the nicest women she ever knew even if she was her sister.

1 Mother's nickname for dad was Os, as though a shortened form of Oscar. I never knew where she came up with that. When doing research, I discovered on census records that dad's middle name was Arthur. As a 3 year old, dad's first name was Rufus. First I knew of this. Perhaps only his wife and his mama knew his name.

Was the nickname "Os" mother's subtle way of reminding dad that she shared his secret? Mother was not above saying "You remember I know your REAL name". They were funny Wish I had known it at the time.

Just a few things I remember when I think of mama,
Frankie Casey Brown

Beverly Brown Hart

A Bit more

Each autumn my husband and I usually tried to take a few days' vacation. He was so good about scheduling vacation near my birthday. He had a sense of humor few people knew about.

One autumn we were driving through Missouri. Weather had turned cold. There had been a few snowflakes. I was thrilled and thought the few flakes were neat. The radio was on in the car and we heard of a bad day on stock market. It is called "Black Friday",

I could not keep quiet "what a beautiful autumn day with snow for a birthday present!"

He replied in his quiet drawl, "Well, I was really thinking about Black Friday being on your birthday. Yep, you have quite a birthday, mom, quite a birthday"

Another autumn trip Max and I were driving through Newton Co, AR just because he knew I loved to go there. I can still remember the orange and yellowish red leaves falling across the highway in front of us. I had put a cassette in the car which was a dulcimer instrumental, Smoky Mountain Revival The day was perfect.

There was road repair being performed on this particular stretch of highway. I thought the men working were exceptionally friendly. As we passed the different crews, the men would lift a hand to wave and smile as we traveled. I mentioned this to Max. He just shrugged his shoulders. That was often his response.

It was after midday and we saw a place to get a bite to eat. He parked the car. I got out and as I walked in front of the car I began to laugh. He turned and said "what is so funny?"

"Don't you see it? That is why everyone has been so friendly!"

"See what?"

"Look at the bumper on front of car." The car had a tag on it when we bought the car. It was promoting our home town of Pryor, OK. It had one word on it, Pryor. I said "who is governor of Arkansas? Governor Pryor"

"Those workmen think you are the governor or one of his men! Guess what? If you are the governor; that means I am the first lady!"

He smiled and said, "well, trust me, I am not the governor and you surely are not the first lady"

He had done it again. Dashed my dreams! We had hard times, but ohhh we had a lot of fun!

I miss you, every day, I miss you; not the man I married. But I miss the man you became; always protective, supportive, fierce champion of your sons and grandchildren.

I remember when he stopped smoking cigarettes. He told me he had smoked since he was 12 years old. He had smoked for more than 25 years. The friendly men at the nearby convenience store called him "the Winston Man". Max just decided this was not what he should be doing. The Lord had been dealing with him about the addiction habit. He laid the cigarettes down one day. He said he missed putting his hand to his shirt pocket to get a cigarette as much or more than the nicotine withdrawal.

Yes I miss the man you became with all my heart.

When I get lonely I think of you in a land that knows no loneliness or pain. That is when thankfulness far outweighs sadness.

My prayer is that each of our family, some are biological some are by choice, live in homes that are Colonies of Heaven. That is possible only when God is the Head of their Home.

Yes, I pray every day that Eternity will be with those I love on earth. I'm doing it again. Talking to my husband and he isn't here. Or is he? I will ask him some day.

Gymnasium   Teacherage   Academy

William Uriah Casey helped establish this extraordinary school. His son was Jesse Columbus Casey. Daughters of Jesse Columbus and Margaret Houston Casey attended country schools through 8th grade. Each of the girls, Floy, Faye, and Frankie, graduated from the Academy. Picture belonged to mother Frankie Casey Brown.

Mt Parthenon, Newton Co Academy...The school, gymnasium, dormitory
Mother, Frankie Casey, graduated 1929

ANTHONY CASEY—DESCENDANTS

Anthony Casey
b. Dec 29, 1826 Tennessee
m. Mahala Celia Self
d. Sep 26, 1910 Newton Co, AR

Son William Uriah Casey
b. Apr 16, 1849
m. 1. Mary Elizabeth Carlton
d. Apr 05, 1925 Newton Co, AR

Grandson Jesse Columbus Casey
b. Apr 1877
m. Margaret Ann Houston
d. May 21, 1946

Great Granddaughter Frankie Casey
b. October 12, 1912
m. Arthur T Brown
d. Nov 18, 1975

Great Great Granddaughter Beverly J Brown
b. October 19, 1945
m. Max R. Hart Sr
d. living

1 Gr Gr Gr Grandson
Max R Hart Jr   m. Kathy Rupe

Gr Gr Gr Gr Grson Franklin Arthur Hart
m. Regina Fletcher

2. Gr Gr Gr Grandson
Justin Wade Hart   m. Ashley Polk
Gr Gr Gr Gr Granddaughter Ella Grace Hart

JOHN CASPER HOUNSHELL—DESCENDANTS

John Casper Hounshell
b. @ 1730 Germany
m.Christina Messersmith
d.Aug. 1810 Wythe Co, VA

Son Andrew Hounshell
b. October, 1766 Dauphin, PA . . . .
m. Louise Lambert
d.@ 1832 Wythe Co, VA . . . .

Granddaughter Christina Hounshell
b. Feb 28, 1796 Rural Retreat Wythe Co VA
m. Isham Brown
d. July 17, 1875 Boyd Co KY

Great Grandson John Brown
b. @ 1815 West Virginia
m. Matilda Jane Carter
$^{m\ 2}$ Amanda Rucker
d. Aug. 05, 1894 Boyd Co KY

Great Great Grandson Andrew Brown
b. July, 1842 Virginia
m. Martha Fields
$^{m.1}$. Mattocks
d. 1901-1907 Vicinity Little Kansas, OK

Great Great Great Grandson John Wesley Brown
b. Feb 13, 1879 Old Alluwe, I or (MO)
m. Victoria Arella Tilton
d. Feb 26, 1950 Vinita, OK

Great Great Great Great Grandson Arthur T Brown
b. July 10, 1907 Old Alluwe, Indian Territory
m. Frankie Casey
d. February, 1974 Nowata, OK

Great Great Great Great Granddaughter Beverly Jean Brown
b. October 19 1945
m. Max R Hart Sr

THOMAS HOUSTON—DESCENDANTS

Thomas Houston
b.1805 SC or Tennessee
m. Sarah Henson
d. Sep 1860 AR

Son Harvey H Houston
b. Mar o4, 1844 Georgia
m. Harriett Blackwood
d. Aug 05, 1907 Maud, OK

Granddaughter Margaret A Houston
b. July 13, 1874
Newton Co AR
m. Jesse Columbus Casey
d. Jan 16, 1922 Parthenon, AR

Gr Granddaughter Frankie Casey . . . .
b. October 12, 1912
Newton Co AR
m. Arthur T Brown
d. November 18, 1975 Nowata, OK

Great Great Granddaughter Beverly Jean Brown
b. October 19, 1945
m. Max R Hart Sr

MORE ABOUT the Tilton FAMILY

My Father's Arthur T Brown) family

Joseph Tilton
b Jan 11, 1841 in Ohio

[m1] Sada Dines Joseph and Sada Dines had a daughter Luese or Lou Tilton Lou m. James J Sisney.
This family lived at "Old Alluwe", OK They are buried at relocated Ketchum (now Winganon) cemetery near New Alluwe. (My dad told me that Lou Sisney was his mother's half sister)

[m2] Mary Adams
Joseph Tilton and Mary Adams had children
James Tilton b @ 1868
Anson Ellsworth b @ 1869
Ephraim Hosea b @ 1870
Mannford b Sep 2, 1873
Nora b 1882
Caleb Chaplin b Feb 12, 1885
Alonzo Tilton b. 1886
Esther b 1888

The youngest was Victoria Arella Tilton
b. Jan 12, 1890
d. May 09, 1956.
She married John Wesley Brown.
Vic and Wes Brown had children incl Arthur T Brown.

[m3] Jennie Douthet no issue

VIC AND WES BROWN HAD CHILDREN

Arthur T Brown
b. July 10, 1907 Old Alluwe Indian Territory
m. Frankie Casey

Teddy Alford Brown
b 1908 d 1908.
My dad told me this wee babe was born, died, and ma buried the baby while Wes was away on a hunting trip. Buried at relocated Ketchum (now Winganon) cemetery

Joseph Harmon Brown
b. June 27, 1910.
d. Feb 24, 1925
auto pedestrian accident on highway 28 N of "Old Alluwe" OK. Buried at relocated Ketchum (now Winganon) cemetery.

Lula Mattie Brown
m. Ollie Triplett
b. Jan 11, 1915.
d. Oct 12, 1962 buried at Sperry, OK.

Marry Fannie Brown
m. Howard Quigley
b. Feb 05, 1920
d. Nob 13, 1990 Buried Chelsea City cemetery

Pauline Brown
b. Jan 02, 1922
d. Apr 05, 1987
m. Melvin Chester Hull.
Pauline is buried at relocated Ketchum (now Winganon) cemetery.

Dennis McEllery Brown
b. Aug 03, 1032
d. 1962 in auto accident in PA.
m. Darlene unknown.
Had one son. I saw this family one time when they came to visit us. The little boy was called Dusty. I have tried to locate this boy (now a man) but have never located him. My "brick wall".

Mamie the doll with three faces is awake. Next is mother's cotton cards, make do pin cushion, made from broken kerosene lamp base. These are sitting on cotton bedspread woven by Margaret Houston Casey. Jesse and Margaret Casey planted the cotton, chopped it, carded it. Margaret spun into thread on a spinning wheel before weaving on a loom to make a bed spread.

Mamie cotton cards pin cushion

The doll with three faces is Mamie. Mother made her dress and socks. The socks were once the top of dad's work socks. Mamie was given to me @ 1952 by Mamie Williams. Mamie and EJ had no children, but they loved them. Mother and dad were neighbors to EJ and Mamie when I was less than 1 year old. Their friendship remained as long as they lived. The doll had belonged to Mamie for many years. Mamie Williams would be over 125 years old today. EJ signed as witness for dad's voter registration. See pg. 28

The cotton cards and make do pin cushion belonged to mother, Frankie Casey Brown. Pin cushion was a kerosene lamp in a former life. The bedspread is coverlet referenced in sketch "Woman Plain and Simple ~ Secret she kept 40 years.

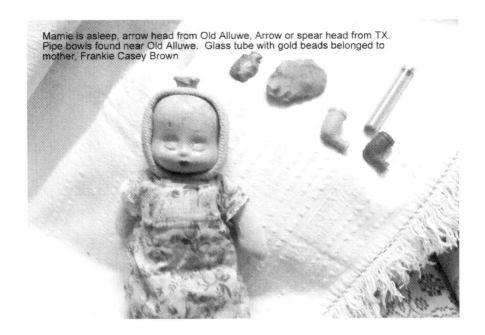
Mamie is asleep, arrow head from Old Alluwe, Arrow or spear head from TX. Pipe bowls found near Old Alluwe. Glass tube with gold beads belonged to mother, Frankie Casey Brown

Mamie arrow hed pipe bowls glass tube

Mamie, the doll, is asleep here. Her three faces are awake, asleep, and crying.

Back of Mamie: L to R: Arrow head found by dad near Old Alluwe on old Indian Camp Ground. Arrow or Spear head found by Max Hart SR in north Texas. His guide thought they were standing on or near where ancestor John Hart was killed in gun fight. Clay Pipe bowls were found by dad near old Alluwe in vicinity of old Indian Camp Ground. Glass tube full of tiny gold colored beads belonged to mother, Frankie Casey Brown. Antiques Road Show said tiny beads are indeed gold. Mother had this as long as I remember, probably since before she married.